uncovered editions

Titles in the series

uncovered editions

THE BOER WAR: LADYSMITH AND MAFEKING, 1900

London: The Stationery Office

First published 1901 Cd. 457 & 458, 1902 Cd. 463, Cd. 968
& Cd. 987
© Crown Copyright

This abridged edition
© The Stationery Office 1999
Reprinted with permission.

ISBN 0 11 702408 2

A CIP catalogue record for this book is available from the
British Library.

Printed in the UK by Biddles Limited, Guildford, Surrey
J93484   C50   11/99

Uncovered Editions are historic official papers which have not previously been available in a popular form. The series has been created directly from the archive of The Stationery Office in London, and the books have been chosen for the quality of their story telling. Some subjects are familiar, but others are less well known. Each is a moment of history.

The British Empire went to war against the Boers in South Africa in October 1899. Within a few weeks the two main British forces were beseiged in the towns of Ladysmith and Mafeking, and a huge army was shipped from England to rescue them. These papers are the despatches to London from the commanders in the field.

The Boer War - Ladysmith under siege, 1899-1900

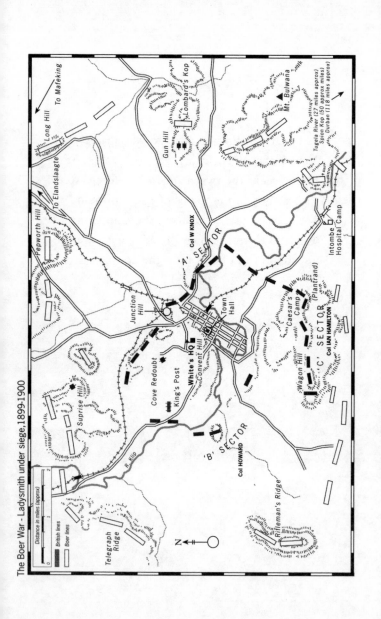

PART ONE

⚜

DESPATCHES RELATING TO THE SIEGE AND RELIEF OF LADYSMITH

SOUTH AFRICA DESPATCHES

NATAL FIELD ARMY

From General Sir Redvers Buller to the Secretary of State for War.
(Through the Field-Marshal Commanding-in-Chief, Cape Town.)

Spearman's Hill Camp,
Sir,   2nd February, 1900.

I have the honour to forward a despatch from Lieut.-General Sir George White, which I have only just received by runner. It is in continuation of his despatch of the 2nd November, 1899, and it will be seen that it deals only with his operations up to 30th October, 1899.

It may, therefore, I think, be inferred that the services of the Officers, non-commissioned officers and men which he brings to notice were rendered by them prior to that date.

I have the honour to be,
Sir,
Your obedient Servant,
REDVERS BULLER, *General.*
Jacobsdal,

Secretary of State for War.   18th February 1900.
Forwarded.
ROBERTS, *Field-Marshal, Commanding-in-Chief,*
South Africa.

From Lieut.-General Sir George White, V.C., G.C.B., G.C.S.I., G.C.I.E., Commanding the British Forces in Natal, to the Secretary of State for War.
(Through the General Officer Commanding in South Africa.)

Sir,   Ladysmith, Natal, 2nd December, 1899.
In continuation of my despatch of 2nd November, 1899, I have now the honour to report

the occurrences of 24th October, referred to briefly in the last paragraph of my above-mentioned despatch. On that date I marched out of Ladysmith at dawn with the 5th Lancers, 19th Hussars, Imperial Light Horse, Natal Mounted Volunteers, 42nd and 53rd Batteries, Royal Field Artillery; No. 10 Mountain Battery, Royal Garrison Artillery; 1st Bn. Liverpool Regiment, 1st Bn. Devonshire Regiment, 1st Bn. Gloucestershire Regiment, and 2nd Bn. King's Royal Rifle Corps. The mounted troops were sent on in advance, and, after going about 6 miles along the Newcastle Road, came under rifle fire from the hills on their left on Rietfontein Farm. The 19th Hussars pushed on over the Modder Spruit and seized and held a ridge about 2 miles beyond that stream by dismounted fire, while watching the country to the front and flanks with patrols. The 5th Lancers similarly seized and held ridges south of the Modder Spruit, as also did the Imperial Light Horse. By this disposition of the mounted troops my right flank was entirely protected during the subsequent action.

At 8 a.m. I arrived at Rietfontein at the head of the main body. At this moment the enemy opened artillery fire on my advanced Cavalry from a point high up on the Intintanyone Mountain, and about 5,000 yards to the west of the main road, at which he had apparently posted four guns. My Artillery was at once ordered to wheel off the road and come into action against these guns, which opened fire on them, but were quickly silenced. Leaving the 2nd Bn. King's Royal Rifle Corps with the baggage wagons, I moved the remainder of the Infantry under the shelter of a high ridge, parallel to the road, and facing the Intintanyone Mountain. The 1st Bn. Gloucestershire Regiment on the left, and the 1st Bn. Liverpool Regiment on the right were then advanced to the crest of this ridge, the Artillery also advancing and coming into action on the crest line between these two regiments. The position thus attained was one most suitable to my purpose, which was to prevent the enemy moving to the east, across the Newcastle Road, and attacking Brigadier-General Yule's force during its retirement from Dundee.

Our Artillery was entirely successful in preventing the enemy from making any further use of his guns, but a severe fire fight gradually developed between my troops and the enemy's infantry, and it became necessary to push the 1st Bn. Devonshire Regiment also to the crest of the ridge, half the 2nd Bn. King's Royal Rifle Corps being brought up from the wagons to take their place in reserve. In this Infantry fight our Artillery rendered great assistance, searching out the crest line and reverse slopes of the opposing ridges most effectively, and thus keeping down the enemy's rifle fire. Mean-while the Natal Mounted Volunteers, who had been with the Cavalry, had been recalled, and, as the enemy showed some disposition to work round my left flank, as if to cut me from Ladysmith, I sent this force, under Colonel Royston, to work round the Boer right and cover my left flank, a movement which was most successfully performed. It was no part of my plan to deliver an attack on the enemy, posted as he was in ground exceptionally well suited to his tactics, and especially difficult for our troops; I contented myself, therefore, with maintaining the position I had gained. The Boers, on the other hand, were unwilling to attack us expect by fire at long ranges, and as they could not approach Brigadier-General Yule's force without doing so, they gradually withdrew to the westward. By 2 p.m. firing had ceased, and as time had now been afforded for the Dundee column to pass the point of danger I returned with my troops to Ladysmith. Our casualties consisted of one Officer and 11 non-commissioned officers and men killed, six Officers and 97 non-commissioned officers and men wounded, and two non-commissioned officers and men missing. The enemy's loss was heavy, particularly from artillery fire.

On 25th October I sent out a force, under Lieut.-Colonel Coxhead, R.A., to meet and, if necessary, to assist Brigadier-General Yule. This force got touch with the Dundee column that afternoon, and, as already reported, both columns reached Ladysmith next morning (26th October) without any interference from the enemy.

On 27th, 28th and 29th October the enemy gradually approached Ladysmith from the west, north, and north-east. These days were spent by us in reconnaissances with a view to finding a favourable opportunity to strike a blow at him. On 29th October our Cavalry located a considerable Boer force with artillery on Long Hill, north-east of

Ladysmith, and well within striking distance. I accordingly issued orders for an attack next day, which resulted in the action of Lombard's Kop.

My object was, in the first instance, to carry Long Hill, and, in the event of success, to similarly carry Pepworth's Hill, sending, at the same time, a considerable mounted force round over Nicholson's Nek to cut the enemy's line of retreat and endeavour to capture his laagers. To gain these objects I employed the entire force assembled at Ladysmith. 200 Natal Mounted Volunteers were sent out the evening before to hold Lombard's Kop and Bulwana Mountain. The 5th Lancers, 19th Hussars, and the remainder of the Natal Mounted Volunteers were ordered to move out, under Major-General French, at 3 a.m. on 30th October, cross Lombard's Nek and the Modder Spruit and cover my right flank during the operations. A Brigade Division of Royal Field Artillery, the Natal Field Battery, 1st and 2nd Bns. King's Royal Rifle Corps, 1st Bn. Leicestershire Regiment, 1st Bn. Liverpool Regiment, and 2nd Bn. Royal Dublin Fusiliers, the whole under Colonel Grimwood, King's Royal Rifle Corps, were detailed for the attack on Long Hill, moving at night so as to be ready to commence the attack at dawn. An infantry Brigade, under Colonel Ian Hamilton, C.B., D.S.O., consisting of 2nd Bn. Gordon Highlanders, 1st Bn. Manchester Regiment, 1st Bn. Devonshire Regiment, and 2nd Bn. Rifle Brigade, together with the Divisional Troops, consisting of a Brigade Division, Royal Artillery 5th Dragoon Guards, 18th

Hussars, Imperial Light Horse, and two companies, Mounted Infantry, were directed to rendezvous at the railway crossing on the Newcastle Road, and proceed to take up a position under cover of Limit Hill. This latter Brigade Division was directed, in the first instance, to assist in shelling Long Hill, the Infantry being intended for the attack on Pepworth's Hill. To cover my left flank and open a way for the action of the Cavalry after the position had been carried, No. 10 Mountain Battery, the 1st Bn. Royal Irish Fusiliers, and the 1st Bn. Gloucestershire Regiment, the whole under Lieut.-Colonel F. Carleton, Royal Irish Fusiliers, with Major W. Adye, D.A.A.G., for Intelligence, as Staff Officer and Guide, were directed to fall in, at 11 p.m., on 29th October, and make a night march up Bell's Spruit to seize as strong a position as could be obtained towards Nicholson's Nek; if possible, the Nek itself.

The troops moved out in accordance with these instructions. The mounted troops, under General French, passed between Lombard's Kop and Bulwana Mountain, but failed to penetrate further than the line of kopjes north-east of the Nek, where at day-break they came under the fire of the enemy's guns and rifles. They held the enemy in check here but could not advance further. The Infantry Brigade, under Colonel Grimwood, reached their appointed position, and the Artillery opened on Long Hill, which, however, was found to have been evacuated by the enemy during the night. At this moment Colonel Grimwood's force was attacked by guns and mounted infantry in large numbers from beyond the Modder Spruit, and had to change front to the right to meet this development, as the Cavalry, having been unable to get beyond the kopjes north-east of Lombard's Nek, were not in a position to cover that flank. Gradually the enemy's numbers increased, and made continual efforts to turn both flanks of the position occupied by Colonel Grimwood's force, necessitating a constant prolongation of his fighting line, and thus using up his supports and reserves, which, by 10 a.m., had all been absorbed in the firing line. Meanwhile artillery fire had been opened by the enemy from Pepworth Hill, one of the guns employed being a 15-cm. gun, throwing a shell of about 100 lbs. weight, which commenced firing on the town of Ladysmith at a range of 8,000 yards. These guns were silenced by our Field Artillery, which also drove the enemy from the crest of Pepworth Hill. It was now about 8 a.m. At this period Major-General French reported that he was holding his position with difficulty against superior forces of the enemy, and I detached the 5th Dragoon Guards and 18th Hussars, under Brigadier-General Brocklehurst, to his assistance; the 69th and 21st Field Batteries being also moved to his support, and with this assistance he easily held his own till the end of the action. Of the remaining batteries, the 13th and 53rd were engaged in supporting Colonel Grimwood's force, while the 42nd and 67th were still firing on Pepworth Hill, from which the enemy had reopened fire, while he had also brought fresh guns on to Long Hill.

About 10 a.m. I withdrew the Manchester Regiment from Colonel Hamilton's force and placed it in a position to support Colonel Grimwood. The fight now became stationary, our troops holding their positions without any great difficulty, but being unable to advance. The Boers, on the other hand, were unable to make any headway. This condition of affairs continued until 11.30 a.m., when, finding that there was little prospect of bringing the engagement to a decisive issue, I determined to withdraw my troops. I accordingly moved the 2nd Bn. Gordon Highlanders from my left to a strong position on Flag Hill, and sent Major-General Sir A. Hunter, K.C.B., my Chief of the Staff, to arrange a retirement in echelon from the left, covered by the fire of our Artillery. This was most successfully carried out, the Artillery advancing in the most gallant manner and covering the Infantry movement with the greatest skill and coolness.

Meanwhile the Naval Brigade landed from H.M.S. "Powerful," which had reached Ladysmith that morning, under Captain Hon. H. Lambton, R.N., had moved out with their long 12-pr. guns on improvised field mountings, drawn by oxen, and had engaged the enemy's artillery on Pepworth Hill, directing their special attention to the heavy gun mounted there, which they temporarily silenced. The enemy did not follow up our retirement, and the whole force employed on this side returned to camp at 1.30 p.m.

Turning now to this force, consisting of No. 10 Mountain Battery, Royal Irish Fusiliers, and the

Gloucestershire Regiment, under Lieut.-Colonel F. Carleton, Royal Irish Fusiliers, which proceeded by a night march up Bell's Spruit towards Nicholson's Nek to cover my left flank, I regret that, owing to the circumstances about to be related, I have no official report of their movements. My information has been obtained from subordinate Officers, who, being severely wounded, were sent into my camp here by General Joubert. From this information it appears that the force moved off, as ordered, at 11 p.m. on 29th October, and proceeded for some distance without seeing signs of the enemy. When passing along the foot of a steep hill, known as Cainguba, stones were suddenly rolled down on them and some shots were fired. The Infantry at once fixed bayonets and carried the hill without difficulty, but unfortunately both the Mountain Battery mules and those carrying the Infantry ammunition took fright and stampeded. Mules carrying two guns eventually returned to camp, one was retained with the force, but no trace has been found of the other three, which presumably fell into the enemy's hands.

The force took up a position on Cainguba, which they strengthened with breastworks to some slight extent, and remained unmolested till daybreak. It was then found that the position was too large for them to adequately occupy, and that only the most pronounced salients could be held. The Boers appear to have gradually surrounded the hill, and after a fight extending over several hours, our men's ammunition began to fail owing to the ammunition mules having stampeded, as already described. The advanced parties holding the salients were driven back on the main body in the centre of the plateau, and the Boers gained the crest line of the hill, whence they brought a converging fire to bear from all sides on our men crowded together in the centre, causing much loss. Eventually it was seen that this position was hopelessly untenable, and our force hoisted a white flag and surrendered about 12.30 p.m.

Including under the head of "missing" those thus taken prisoners, our losses this day amounted to six Officers and 63 non-commissioned officers and men killed, 10 Officers and 239 non-commissioned officers and men wounded, and 37 Officers and 917 non-commissioned officers and men missing.

Next day, 31st October, General Sir Redvers Buller, V.C., G.C.B., &c., arrived at Cape Town, and assumed the command in the whole of South Africa. My independent command in Natal consequently came to an end, and I therefore close this Despatch with the events of 30th October. Subsequent events will be reported to the General Officer Commanding in South Africa in the ordinary course.

I desire to place on record my gratitude to the Government of Natal, and to all departments under the Government, for the most willing and hearty assistance which they have afforded me in every matter in which their co-operation was required.

II

From Field-Marshal Lord Roberts to the Secretary of State for War.

Sir   20th February, 1901

I have the honour to submit for your information a Despatch, dated Camp Springfield, 8th February, 1900, from General Sir Redvers. Buller, Commanding in Natal, giving an account of the operations between the 25th January and the 7th February. I regret that, through some mistake, the despatch was not forwarded to you at the time.

I have, &c.,
ROBERTS, Field-Marshal.

Camp Springfield,

Sir, 8th February, 1900.

I have the honour to report that on the 25th ultimo, as already reported, I decided it was desirable to withdraw my force from the west of Spion Kop. While they had been there, the enemy had very considerably strengthened his right, so that any attempt to advance our left would probably have been unsuccessful, while the failure to hold Spion Kop proved the strength of the enemy in front of our right.

I therefore withdrew the force and commenced preparations for a trial by another route. These preparations involved the formation of a road to the top of a very precipitous hill and the occupation of its summit by guns. Unfortunately the weather was very unpropitious and seriously retarded this work. Begun on the 27th, by the evening of the 3rd February it was completed—about 1½ miles of road through a very difficult country having been made up a steep hillside, and six naval 12-pr., two 15-pr. Royal Field Artillery, and six mountain battery Royal Artillery guns having been got to the top.

Unfortunately, the weather was too bad to admit of our getting up the two 5-inch guns which we had hoped to mount there. I must bear witness to the admirable way in which the Naval Brigade, the Royal Artillery, the Royal Engineers, and the Royal Scots Fusiliers worked at this arduous duty.

In the absence of any Officer Commanding Royal Artillery in Natal, I asked Majors Findlay and Apsley Smith, Royal Artillery, to advise me as to the best positions for the various guns at my disposal, and was much obliged by their advice.

The demonstration in front of Brakfontein was very well made by the 11th Brigade under General Wynne. The men in their extreme keenness got rather closer to the positions than I had wished, but though a very heavy fire both of shell and rifle was opened upon them, they retired when ordered in admirable order and with, I am thankful to say, but slight loss.

The batteries were also under heavy fire, the men fighting their guns as coolly as if on parade: their loss, fortunately, was small.

As soon as sufficient time had been given to get the Brakfontein trenches fully occupied, the batteries moved in succession from the left to the right over No. 2 Pontoon Bridge which had been constructed the night before, and the 4th Brigade under General Lyttelton supported by the 2nd Division advanced under cover of their fire to cover the construction of No. 3 Pontoon (6661) Bridge which was well and rapidly thrown under a well directed but long range fire.

As soon as it was completed the 2nd Durham Light Infantry supported by the 1st Rifle Brigade advanced on Vaal Krantz under a heavy fire from the hill and the dongas on the right, causing considerable loss, but the men would not be denied and the position was soon taken. It was later on occupied by the whole of the 4th Brigade, Mungers Farm being occupied by a battalion of the 2nd Brigade. The position thus gained was held till the following morning.

On the 6th, No. 2 Pontoon Bridge was taken up and reconstructed at the back of Vaal Krantz instead, to facilitate communication.

I should have mentioned that Vaal Krantz was occupied by a gun and some 120 of the enemy, of these the Field Cornet in charge went off with about half and the gun as we approached, most of the rest were killed by our shell and infantry fire, but we took six prisoners. I am sorry to have to report that among the men on the hill were several armed kaffirs—Lieutenant Lambton of the Durham Light Infantry was wounded by one—and during the day we had ocular demonstration that the stories we had heard of the enemy arming natives to fight against us are not untrue.

We also all saw a gun detachment, and we thought the gun also, conveyed by the enemy to a gun position in an ambulance flying the Geneva flag.

On the evening of the 6th I relieved the 4th Brigade on Vaal Krantz by the 2nd Brigade, and all that and the following day I endeavoured to entrench a position on the hill but found the ground too rocky.

It was also raked by two guns which none of mine could silence, a 75 mm. Creusot on Spion Kop, and a 15 cm. Creusot on the top of the hill above Doorn Kloof. The first they could not see, the second was on a sort of truck mounting, its muzzle showed up when it fired and then it disappeared. Our 4.7, 12-pr. Naval, and 5-inch guns fired at it for the two days, they twice blew up its magazine or ammunition store, but failed to silence the gun.

As the safe tenure of Vaal Krantz was indispensable for further operations, and I could neither entrench there owing to the extremely rocky nature of the ground, nor protect it from Artillery fire, I concluded that an advance by that route would be impossible, and, recalling the 2nd Brigade at sunset, determined to try another passage.

As an illustration of the nature of the country I may mention that on the 5th the enemy were bringing what appeared to be a Maxim Norden-feldt gun drawn by eight horses on a galloping carriage across the back of the position from West to East—as they crossed the Mungers Farm—Klipport Road, they came under the fire of our guns on Swartz Kop. The first shell went very close, and the team turned sharp to the right and disappeared, they seemed to have fallen over into a donga, a shell followed them in, and we saw no more of them till they reappeared at least a mile off out of another donga, short of two horses and a man. The country was honeycombed with these dongas, all of which had been utilised for defence.

Of the prisoners we took, two, an Austrian and an Englishman, belonged to the Johannesburg Commando. They described their Commando as a mixture of all nationalities under the sun except Dutch, the common language being English. One of them said that in Johannesburg alone there were now over 2,000 widows who still believed their husbands to be alive.

III

From Field-Marshal Lord Roberts to the Secretary of State for War

Army Head-quarters, South Africa,
Camp, Dekiel Drift, Riet River,

My Lord,   13th February, 1900.

I have the honour to submit, for your Lordship's information, despatches from General Sir Redvers Buller, describing the advance across the Tugela River on the 17th and 18th January, 1900, and the capture and evacuation of the Spion Kop position on the 23rd and 24th January, as well as certain minor operations between the 19th and 24th January on the right or eastern line of advance.

The plan of operations is not very clearly described in the despatches themselves, but it may be gathered from them and the accompanying documents themselves that the original intention was to cross the Tugela at or near Trichard's Drift, and thence by following the road past "Fair View" and "Acton Homes," to gain the open plain north of Spion Kop, the Boer position in front of Potgieter's Drift being too strong to be taken by direct attack. The whole force, less one brigade, was placed under the orders of Sir Charles Warren, who, the day after he had crossed the Tugela, seems to have consulted his General and principal Staff Officers, and to have come to the conclusion that the flanking movement which Sir Redvers Buller had mentioned in his secret instructions was impracticable on account of the insufficiency of supplies. He accordingly decided to advance by the more direct road leading north-east, and branching off from a point east of "Three Tree Hill." The selection of this road necessitated the capture and retention of Spion Kop, but whether it would have been equally necessary to occupy Spion Kop, had the line of advance indicated by Sir Redvers Buller been followed, is not stated in the correspondence. As Sir Charles Warren considered it impossible to make the wide flanking movement which was recommended, if not actually prescribed, in his secret instructions, he should at once have acquainted Sir Redvers Buller with the course of action which he proposed to adopt. There is nothing to show whether he did so or not, but it seems only fair to Sir Charles Warren to point out that Sir Redvers Buller appears throughout to have been aware of what was happening. On several occasions he was present during the operations. He repeatedly gave advice to his subordinate Commander, and on the day after the withdrawal from Spion Kop he resumed the chief command.

In his note on Sir Charles Warren's report, accompanying despatch of 30th January, 1900, Sir Redvers Buller expresses a very adverse opinion on the manner in which Sir Charles Warren carried out the instructions he had received. Without a knowledge of the country and circumstances it is difficult to say whether the delay, misdirection, and want of control, of which Sir Redvers Buller complains, were altogether avoidable; but, in any case, if he considered that his orders were not being properly given effect to, it appears to me that it was his duty to intervene as soon as he had reason to believe that the success of the operations was being endangered. This, indeed, is admitted by Sir Redvers Buller himself, whose explanation of his non-interference can hardly be accepted as adequate. A most important enterprise was being attempted, and no personal considerations should have deterred the Officer in chief command from insisting on its being conducted in the manner to which, in his opinion, would lead to the attainment of the object in view, with the least possible loss on our side.

As regards the withdrawal of the troops from the Spion Kop position, which, though occupied almost without opposition in the early morning of the 24th January, had to be held throughout the day under an extremely heavy fire, and the retention of which had become essential to the relief of Ladysmith, I regret that I am unable to concur with Sir Redvers Buller in thinking that Lieut.-Colonel Thorneycroft exercised a wise discretion in ordering the troops to retire. Even admitting that due preparations may not have been made for strengthening the position during the night, reorganizing the defence, and bringing up artillery— in regard to which Sir Charles Warren's report does not altogether bear our Sir Redvers Buller's contention—admitting also that the senior Officers on the summit of the hill might have been more promptly informed of the measures taken by Sir Charles Warren to support and reinforce them, I am of opinion that Lieut.-Colonel Thorneycroft's assumption of responsibility and authority was wholly inexcusable. During the night the enemy's fire, if it did not cease altogether, could not have been formidable, and, though lamp signalling was not possible at the time, owing to the supply of oil having failed, it would not have taken more than two or three hours at most for Lieut.-Colonel Thorneycroft to communicate by messenger with Major-General Coke or Sir Charles Warren, and to receive a reply. Major-General Coke appears to have left Spion Kop at 9.30 p.m. for the purpose of consulting with Sir Charles Warren, and up to that hour the idea of a withdrawal had not been entertained. Yet almost immediately after Major-General Coke's departure Lieut.-Colonel Thorneycroft issued an order, without reference to superior authority, which upset the whole plan of operations, and rendered unavailing the sacrifices which had already been made to carry it into effect.

On the other hand, it is only right to state that Lieut.-Colonel Thorneycroft appears to have behaved in a very gallant manner throughout the day, and it was doubtless due, in a great measure, to his exertions and example that the troops continued to hold the summit of the hill until directed to retire.

The conduct of Captain Phillips, Brigade-Major of the 10th Brigade, on the occasion in question, is deserving of high commendation. He did his best to rectify the mistake which was being made, but it was too late. Signalling communication was not re-estab-lished until 2.30 a.m. on the 25th January, and by that time the Naval guns could not have reached the summit of the hill before daybreak. Major-General Coke did not return, and Lieut.-Colonel Thorneycroft had gone away. Moreover, most of the troops had begun to leave the hill, and the working parties, with the half company of Royal Engineers, had also withdrawn.

It is to be regretted that Sir Charles Warren did not himself visit Spion Kop during the afternoon or evening, knowing as he did that the state of affairs there was very critical, and that the loss of the posi-tion would involve the failure of the operations. He was, consequently, obliged to summon Major-

General Coke to his head-quarters in the evening in order that he might ascertain how matters were going on, and the command on Spion Kop thus devolved on Lieut.-Colonel Thorneycroft; but Major-General Coke was not aware of this. About mid-day, under instructions from Sir Redvers Buller, Sir Charles Warren had directed Lieut.-Colonel Thorneycroft to assume command on the summit of the hill, with the temporary rank of Brigadier-General, but this order was not communicated to Major-General Coke, who, until he left the position at 9.30 p.m., was under the impression that the command had devolved on Colonel Hill, as senior Officer, after Colonel Crofton had been wounded. Omissions or mistakes of this nature may be trivial in themselves, yet may exercise an important influence on the course of events; and I think that Sir Redvers Buller is justified in remarking that "there was a want of organization and system which acted most unfavourably on the defence."

The attempt to relieve Ladysmith, described in these despatches, was well devised, and I agree with Sir Redvers Buller in thinking that it ought to have succeeded. That it failed may, in some measure, be due to the difficulties of the ground and the commanding positions held by the enemy—probably also to errors of judgment and want of administrative capacity on the part of Sir Charles Warren. But whatever faults Sir Charles Warren may have committed, the failure must also be ascribed to the disinclination of the Officer in supreme command to assert his authority and see that what he thought best was done, and also to the unwarrantable and needless assumption of responsibility by a subordinate Officer.

The gratifying feature in these despatches is the admirable behaviour of the troops throughout the operations.

I have the honour to be,
My Lord,
Your Lordship's most obedient Servant,
ROBERTS, *Field-Marshal,*
Commanding-in-Chief, South Africa.

From General Sir Redvers Buller to the Secretary of State for War.
(Through Field-Marshal Lord Roberts, G.C.B., Commander-in-Chief, Cape Town.)

Spearman's Hill,
Sir,   30th January, 1900.

I have the honour to report that General Sir Charles Warren's Division having arrived at Estcourt, less two battalions, 10th Brigade, which were left at the Cape, by the 7th January, it moved to Free on the 9th.

I attach a copy of Natal Army Orders of the 8th January, giving full particulars of the intended move and organization of the force.

The column moved as ordered, but torrents of rain fell on the 9th, which filled all the spruits, and, indeed, rendered many of them impassable for many hours. To forward supply alone took 650 ox wagons, and as in the 16 miles from Frere to Springfield there were three places at which all the wagons had to be double spanned, and some required three spans, some idea may be formed of the difficulties, but these were all successfully overcome by the willing labours of the troops. I attach a statement of the supply trains.

The 4th Brigade reached Springfield on the 12th, in support of the mounted troops who had surprised and seized the important position of Spearman's Hill, commanding Potgieter's Drift, on the 11th.

By the 13th all troops were at Springfield and Spearman's Hill, and supply was well forward.

On the 16th, a reserve of 17 days' supply having been collected, General Sir C. Warren, in command of the 2nd Division, the 11th Brigade of the 5th Division, the Brigade Division Royal Field Artillery, 5th Division, and certain corps troops, including the Mounted Brigade, moved from Springfield to Trichard's Drift, which is about six miles west of Potgieter's.

I attach a copy of the orders under which Sir C. Warren acted, and enclose his report of his operations.

On the night of the 23rd, General Warren attacked Spion Kop, which operation he has made the subject of a special report. On the morning of the 25th, finding that Spion Kop had been abandoned in the night, I decided to withdraw General Warren's force; the troops had been continuously engaged for a week, in circumstances entailing considerable hardships, there had been very heavy losses on Spion Kop. General Warren's dispositions had mixed up all the brigades, and the positions he held were dangerously insecure. I consequently assumed the command, commenced the withdrawal of the ox and heavy mule transport on the 25th; this was completed by midday the 26th; by double spanning the loaded ox wagons got over the drift at the rate of about eight per hour. The mule wagons went over the pontoon bridge, but all the mules had to be taken out and the vehicles passed over by hand. For about 7 hours of the night the drift could not be used as it was dangerous in the dark, but the use of the pontoon went on day and night. In addition to machine guns, six batteries of Royal Field Artillery, and four howitzers, the following vehicles were passed:—Ox wagons, 232; 10-span mule wagons, 98; 6-span, 107; 4-span, 52; total, 489 vehicles. In addition to these, the ambulances were working backwards and forwards evacuating the sick and wounded.

By 2 p.m., the 26th, all the ox wagons were over, and by 11.30 p.m. all the mule transports were across and the bridge clear for the troops. By 4 a.m., the 27th, all the troops were over, and by 8 a.m. the pontoons were gone and all was clear. The troops had all reached their new camps by 10 a.m. The marches averaged for the mounted troops about 7 miles, and for the Infantry and Artillery an average of 5 miles.

Everything worked without a hitch, and the arrangements reflected great credit on the Staff of all degrees; but I must especially mention Major Irwin, R.E., and his men of the Pontoon Troop, who were untiring. When all men were over, the chesses of the pontoon bridge were so worn by the traffic, that I do not think they would have lasted another half hour.

Thus ended an expedition which I think ought to have succeeded. We have suffered heavily, very heavy losses, and lost many whom we can ill spare; but, on the other hand, we have inflicted as great or greater losses upon the enemy than they have upon us, and they are, by all accounts, thoroughly disheartened; while our troops are, I am glad and proud to say, in excellent fettle.

I have the honour to be,

Sir,

Your obedient Servant,
REDVERS BULLER,
General Officer Commanding.

From General Sir Redvers Buller to Lieut.-General Sir Charles Warren.

Mount Alice,
15th January, 1900.

The enemy's position in front of Potgieter's Drift seems to me to be too strong to be taken by direct attack.

I intend to try and turn it by sending a force across the Tugela from near Trichard's Drift and up to the west of Spion Kop.

You will have command of that force which will consist of the 11th Brigade of your Division, your Brigade Division, Royal Field Artillery, and General Clery's Division complete, and all the mounted troops, except 400.

You will of course act as circumstances require,

but my idea is that you should continue throughout refusing your right and throwing your left forward till you gain the open plain north of Spion Kop. Once there you will command the rear of the position facing Potgieter's Drift, and I think render it untenable.

At Potgieter's there will be the 4th Brigade, part of the 10th Brigade, one battery Royal Field Artillery, one howitzer battery, two 4.7-inch Naval guns. With them I shall threaten both the positions in front of us, and also attempt a crossing at Skiet's Drift, so as to hold the enemy off you as much as possible.

It is very difficult to ascertain the numbers of the enemy with any sort of exactness. I do not think there can be more than 400 on your left, and I estimate the total force that will be opposed to us at about 7,000. I think they have only one or at most two big guns.

You will take 2½ days' supply in your regimental transport, and a supply column holding one day more. This will give you four days' supply which should be enough. Every extra wagon is a great impediment.

I gathered that you did not want an ammunition column. I think myself that I should be inclined to take one column for the two Brigade Divisions. You may find a position on which it is expedient to expend a great deal of ammunition.

You will issue such orders to the Pontoon Troop as you think expedient. If possible, I should like it to come here after you have crossed. I do not think you will find it possible to let oxen draw the wagons over the pontoons. It will be better to draw them over by horses or mules, swimming the oxen; the risk of breaking the pontoons, if oxen cross them, is too great.

The man whom I am sending you as a guide is a Devonshire man; he was employed as a boy on one of my own farms; he is English to the backbone, and can be thoroughly trusted. He thinks that if you cross Springfield flat at night he can take you the rest of the way to the Tugela by a road that cannot be overlooked by the enemy, but you will doubtless have the road reconnoitred.

I shall endeavour to keep up heliographic communication with you from a post on the hill directly in your rear.

I wish you to start as soon as you can. Supply is all in, and General Clery's Division will, I hope, concentrate at Springfield to-day. Directly you start I shall commence to cross the river.

Please send me the 10th Brigade, except that portion which you detail for the garrison at Springfield, as soon as possible; also the eight 12-pr. Naval guns, and any details, such as ammunition column, &c., that you do not wish to take.

REDVERS BULLER, *General.*

From Lieut.-General Sir Charles Warren to the Chief of the Staff.

Hatting's Farm,
Sir,   29th January, 1900.

I have the honour to make the following report on the operations on the north side of the Tugela, west of Spion Kop, from the 17th to the 27th of January, 1900:—

On the 8th January field orders were published constituting the 10th Brigade of the 5th Division a Corps Brigade, and placing the 4th Brigade in the 5th Division. The 5th Division thus constituted marched from Frere on the 10th instant, arriving at Springfield on the 12th instant.

On the 15th January I received your secret instructions to command a force to proceed across the Tugela, near Trichardt's Drift, to the west of Spion Kop, recommending me to proceed forward refusing my right (namely, Spion Kop), and bringing my left forward to gain the open plain north of Spion Kop. This move was to commence as soon as supplies were all in, and the 10th Brigade (except two companies) removed from Springfield Bridge to Spearman's Hill.

I was provided with 4 days' rations, with which I was to cross the Tugela, fight my way round to north of Spion Kop, and join your column opposite Potgieter's.

On the 15th January I made the arrangements for getting supplies, and moved the 10th Brigade on the following day; and on the evening of the 16th January I left Springfield with a force under my command, which amounted to an Army Corps (less one brigade), and by a night march arrived at Trichardt's Drift, and took possession of the hills on the south side of the Tugela.

On the 17th January I threw pontoon bridges across the Tugela, passed the Infantry across by ponts, and captured the hills immediately commanding the drift on the north side with two brigades commanded by Generals Woodgate and Hart. The Commander-in-Chief was present during part of the day, and gave some verbal directions to General Woodgate.

The Mounted Brigade passed over principally by the drift, and went over the country as far as Acton Homes, and on the following day (18th) had a successful action with a small party of Boers, bringing in 31 prisoners.

During the night of the 17th, and day of the 18th, the whole of the wagons belonging to the force were brought across the Tugela, and the artillery were in position outside of Wright's Farm.

On the 19th two brigades advanced, occupying the slopes of the adjoining hills on the right, and the wagons were successfully brought to Venter's Spruit.

In the evening, after having examined the possible roads by which we could proceed, I assembled the General Officers and the Staff, and the Officer Commanding Royal Artillery, and Commanding Royal Engineer, and pointed out to them that of the two roads by which we could advance the eastern one, by Acton Homes, must be rejected, because time would not allow of it, and with this all concurred. I then pointed out that the only possible way of all getting through by the road north of Fair View would be by taking 3 or 4 days' food in our haversacks, and sending all our wagons back across the Tugela; but before we could do this we must capture the position in front of us.

On the following day, 20th January, I placed two brigades and six batteries of Artillery at the disposal of General Sir C. F. Clery, with instructions to attack the Boer positions by a series of outflanking movements, and by the end of the day, after fighting for 12 hours, we were in possession of the whole part of hills, but found a strongly entrenched line on the comparatively flat country beyond us.

On the 21st the Boers displayed considerable activity on our left, and the Commander-in-Chief desired me to move two batteries from right to left. At a subsequent date, during the day, I found it impossible to proceed without howitzers, and telegraphed for four from Potgieter's. These arrived early on the morning of the 22nd, and the Commander-in-Chief, arriving about the same time, directed me to place two of these howitzers on the left, two having already been placed on the right flank. I pointed out to the Commander-in-Chief that it would be impossible to get wagons through by the road leading past Fair View, unless we first took Spion Kop, which lies within about 2,000 yards of the road. The Commander-in-Chief agreed that Spion Kop would have to be taken. Accordingly that evening orders were drawn up giving the necessary instructions to General Talbot Coke to take Spion Kop that night, but, owing to an absence of insufficient reconnaissance, he requested that the attack might be put off for a day.

On the 23rd January the Commander-in-Chief came into camp, the attack on Spion Kop was decided upon, and Lieut.-Colonel àCourt, of the

Head-quarter Staff, was directed by the Commander-in-Chief to accompany General Woodgate, who was detailed to command the attacking column. The account of the capture of Spion Kop is given in another report.

On the morning of the 25th January the Commander-in-Chief arrived, decided to retire the force, and assumed direct command. The whole of the wagons of the 5th Division were got down to the drift during the day, and were crossed over before 2 p.m. on the 26th January.

The arrangements for the retirement of the 5th Division were exceedingly well got out, and the retirement was made in good order during the night of the 26th, the whole of the troops crossing to the south side of the Tugela before daylight, and the wagons were packed, and the troops bivouacked near the spruit about 2 miles to the east of the pontoon bridges. About 10 p.m., previous to the retirement, heavy musketry was heard to the north of our position, which has been attributed to a Boer commando thinking we were going to make a night attack.

I append reports from Lieut.-General Sir C. F. Clery, K.C.B., on the operations conducted by him on the 20th, 21st, and 22nd, also from Major-General Hildyard, C.B., for his operations on those dates.

I propose to forward as soon as possible a more detailed report of the movements of brigades and units, and acts of individuals.

C. WARREN, *Lieut.-General,*
Commanding 5th Division.

Spearman's Camp,

Secretary of State,   30th January, 1900.

In forwarding this report I am constrained to make the following remarks, not necessarily for publication:—

I had fully discussed my orders with General Warren before he started, and he appeared entirely to agree that the policy indicated of refusing the right and advancing the left was the right one. He never though attempted to carry it out. From the first there could be no question but that the only practicable road for his column was the one by Fair View. The problem was to get rid of the enemy who were holding it.

The arrival of the force at Trichard's was a surprise to the enemy, who were not in strength. Sir C. Warren, instead of feeling for the enemy, elected to spend two whole days in passing his baggage. During this time, the enemy received reinforcements and strengthened his position. On the 19th he attacked and gained a considerable advantage. On the 20th, instead of pursuing it, he divided his force, and gave General Clery a separate command.

On the 21st I find that his right was in advance of his left, and that the whole of his batteries, six, were crowded on one small position on his right, while his left was unprotected by Artillery, and I had come out to tell him that the enemy on that flank had received a reinforcement of at least 2,500. I suggested a better distribution of his batteries, which he agreed to, to some extent, but he would not advance his left, and I found that he had divided his fighting line into three independent commands, independent of each other, and apparently independent of him, as he told me he could not move any batteries without General Clery's consent.

The days went on. I saw no attempt on the part of General Warren either to grapple with the situation or to command his force himself. By the 23rd I calculated that the enemy, who were about 600 stong on the 16th, were not less than 15,000, and General White confirmed this estimate. We had really lost our chance by Sir C. Warren's slowness. He seems to me a man who can do well what he can do himself, but who cannot command, as he can use neither his staff nor subordinates. I can never employ him again on an independent command.

On the 19th I ought to have assumed command myself; I saw that things were not going well—indeed, everyone saw that. I blame myself now for not having done so. I did not, because I thought that if I did I should discredit General Warren in the estimation of the troops; and that if I were shot, and he had to withdraw across the Tugela, and they had lost confidence in him, the consequences might be very serious.

I must leave it to higher authority whether this argument was a sound one. Anyhow, I feel convinced that we had a good chance on the 17th, and that we lost it.

REDVERS. BULLER, *General.*

Military Secretary,   30th January, 1900.
    Herewith copy of portions of my despatch which you have called for by telegram.

C. WARREN, *Lieut.-General,*
Commanding 5th Division.

COPY of Instructions issued to Lieut.-General Sir C. F. Clery, dated 19th January, 1900.

General Officer Commanding 2nd Division,
    I shall be glad if you will arrange to clear the Boers out of the ground above that at present occupied by the 11th Brigade, by a series of outflanking movements. In the early morning an advance should be made as far as the Hussars reconnoitred to-day, and a shelter-trench there made across the slope of the hill. A portion of the slopes of the adjoining hill to the west can then be occupied, the Artillery assisting, if necessary, in clearing the western side and upper slopes. When this is done I think that a battery can be placed on the slopes of the western hill in such a position that it could shell the scances of the Boers on Spion Kop and the upper portion of the eastern hill. When this is done a further advance can be made on the eastern hill, and artillery can be brought to bear upon the upper slopes of the western hill. It appears to me that this might be done with comparatively little loss of life, as the Boers can in each turn be outflanked. The following Cavalry are at your disposal—two squadrons Royal Dragoons and 5th Divisional Squadron.

C. WARREN
Lieut. General.

20th January, 1900.

After successfully carrying some of the hills, General Clery reported that he had now reached a point which it would be necessary to take by frontal attack, which he did not think would be desirable.

To this I replied—

"I quite concur that a frontal attack is undesirable, and that a flank attack is more suitable. I intended to convey that we should hold what we get by means of entrenchments when necessary, and not retire, continuing the advance to-morrow if it cannot be done to-night; frontal attack, with heavy losses, is simply playing the Boer game."

C. WARREN.

From the General Officer Commanding, Natal, to the Secretary of State for War.
(By the Field-Marshal Commanding-in-Chief, Cape Town.)

Spearman's Hill,
Sir,   30th January, 1900.

In forwarding Lieut.-General Sir C. Warren's report on the capture and evacuation of Spion Kop, I have the honour to offer the following observations.

Sir C. Warren, is hardly correct in saying that he was only allowed 3½ days' provisions. I had told him that transport for 3½ days would be sufficient burden to him, but that I would keep him filled up as he wanted it. That he was aware of this is shown by the following telegram which he sent on the day in question. It is the only report I had from Sir C. Warren:—

(Sent 7.54 p.m. Received 8.15 p.m.)

"To Chief of the Staff," Left Flank, 19th January.

"I find there are only two roads by which we could possibly get from Trichard's Drift to Potgieter's, on the north of the Tugela—one by Acton Homes, the other by Fair View and Rosalie; the first I reject as too long, the second is a very difficult road for a large number of wagons, unless the enemy is thoroughly cleared out. I am, therefore, going to adopt some special arrangements which will involve my stay at Venter's Laager for 2 or 3 days. I will send in for further supplies and report progress.—C. WARREN."

The reply to this was that 3 days' supply was being sent.

I went over to Sir C. Warren on the 23rd. I pointed out to him that I had no further report and no intimation of the special arrangements foreshadowed by this telegram of the 19th; that for four days he had kept his men continuously exposed to shell and rifle fire, perched on the edge of an almost precipitous hill; that the position admitted of no second line, and the supports were massed close behind the firing line in indefensible formations, and that a panic or a sudden charge might send the whole lot in disorder down the hill at any moment. I said it was too dangerous a situation to be prolonged, and that he must either attack or I should withdraw his force. I advocated, as I had previously done, an advance from his left. He said that he had the night before ordered General Coke to assault Spion Kop, but the latter had objected to undertaking a night attack on a position, the road to which he had not reconnoitred, and added that he intended to assault Spion Kop that night.

I suggested that as General Coke was still lame from the effects of a lately broken leg, General Woodgate, who had two sound legs, was better adapted for mountain climbing.

As no heliograph could, on account of the fire, be kept on the east side of Spion Kop, messages for Sir C. Warren were received by our signallers at Spearman, and telegraphed to Sir C. Warren; thus I saw them before he did, as I was at the signal station. The telegrams Sir C. Warren quotes did not give me confidence in its sender, and, at the moment, I could see that our men on the top had given way, and that efforts were being made to rally them. I telegraphed to Sir C. Warren: "Unless you put some really good hard fighting man in command on the top you will lose the hill. I suggest Thorneycroft."

Colonel à Court was sent down by General Woodgate almost as soon as he gained the summit.

I have not thought it necessary to order any investigation. If at sundown the defence of the summit had been taken regularly in hand, entrenchments laid out, gun emplacements prepared, the dead removed, the wounded collected, and, in fact, the whole place brought under regular military command, and careful arrangements made for the supply of water and food to the scattered fighting line, the hills would have been held, I am sure.

But no arrangements were made. General Coke appears to have been ordered away just as he would have been useful, and no one succeeded him; those on the top were ignorant of the fact that guns were coming up, and generally there was a want of organization and system that acted most unfavourably on the defence.

It is admitted by all that Colonel Thorneycroft acted with the greatest gallantry throughout the day, and really saved the situation. Preparations for the second day's defence should have been organized during the day, and have been commenced at nightfall.

As this was not done, I think Colonel Thorneycroft exercised a wise discretion.

Our losses, I regret to say, were very heavy, but the enemy admitted to our doctors that theirs were equally severe, and though we were not successful in retaining the position, the losses inflicted on the enemy and the attack generally have had a marked effect upon them.

I cannot close these remarks without bearing testimony to the gallant and admirable behaviour of the troops, the endurance shown by the Laucashire Fusiliers, the Middlesex Regiment, and Thorneycroft's Mounted Infantry was admirable, while the efforts of the 2nd Bn. Scottish Rifles and

3rd Bn. King's Royal Rifles were equally good, and the Royal Lancasters fought gallantly.

I am writing to catch the mail, and have not any particulars yet to enable me to report more fully on details.

I have the honour to be,
Sir,
Your obedient Servant,
REDVERS BULLER.

IV

Report by Lieut.-General Sir Charles Warren, K.C.B., upon the Capture and subsequent Evacuation of Spion Kop.

Capture and Evacuation of Spion Kop.

Chief of the Staff,

I make the operations against Spion Kop in a separate report, because they did not enter into my original plans.

Under the original instructions of the General Officer Commanding-in-Chief, of 15th January, 1900, I was to act as circumstances required, but according to instructions, was generally to continue throughout refusing my right, and throwing my left forward until I gained the open plain north of Spion Kop.

Upon the 19th of January, on arrival at Venter's Laager, I assembled all the General Officers, Officers Commanding Royal Artillery and Royal Engineers of Divisions, and Staff Officers together. I pointed out to them that, with the three and a half (3½) days' provisions allowed, it was impossible to advance by the left road through Acton Homes. In this they unanimously concurred. I showed them that the only possible road was that going over Fair View through Rosalie, but I expressed my conviction that this could not be done unless we sent the whole of our transport back across the Tugela, and attempted to march through with our rations in our haversacks—without impedimenta.

The hills were cleared on the following day, and very strong entrenchments found behind them. The Commander-in-Chief was present on the 21st and 22nd January, and I pointed out the difficulties of marching along the road, accompanied by wagons, without first taking Spion Kop.

Accordingly, on the night of the 22nd, I ordered General Coke to occupy Spion Kop. He, however, desired that the occupation might be deferred for a day in order that he might make a reconnaissance with the Officers Commanding battalions to be sent there.

On 23rd January the Commander-in-Chief came into camp, and told me that there were two courses open—(1) to attack, or (2) to retire. I replied that I should prefer to attack Spion Kop to retiring, and showed the Commander-in-Chief my orders of the previous day.

The Commander-in-Chief then desired that I should put General Woodgate in command of the expedition, and detailed Lieut.-Colonel àCourt to accompany him as Staff Officer

The same evening General Woodgate proceeded with the Lancashire Fusiliers, the Royal Lancaster Regiment, a portion of Thorneycroft's Horse, and half company Royal Engineers, supported by two companies of the Connaught Rangers and by the Imperial Light Infantry, the latter having just arrived by Trichardt's Drift.

The attack and capture of Spion Kop was entirely successful. General Woodgate, having secured the summit on the 24th, reported that he had entrenched a position and hoped he was secure, but that the fog was too thick to permit him to see. The position was rushed without casualties, other than three men wounded.

Lieut.-Colonel àCourt came down in the morning and stated that everything was satisfactory and secure, and telegraphed to the Commander-in-Chief to that effect. Scarcely had he started on his return to head-quarters when a heliogram arrived from Colonel Crofton (Royal Lancaster). The message was: "Reinforce at once, or all lost. General dead."

He also sent a similar message to head-quarters. I immediately ordered General Coke to proceed to his assistance, and to take command of the troops. He started at once, and was accompanied by the Middlesex and. Dorsetshire Regiments.

I replied to Colonel Crofton: "I am sending two battalions, and the Imperial Light Infantry are on their way up. You must hold on to the last. No surrender."

This occurred about 10 a.m.

Shortly afterwards I received a telegram from the Commander-in-Chief, ordering me to appoint Lieut.-Colonel Thorneycroft to the command of the summit. I accordingly had heliographed: "With the approval of the Commander-in-Chief, I place Lieut.-Colonel Thorneycroft in command of the summit, with the local rank of Brigadier-General."

For some hours after this message I could get no information from the summit. It appears that the signallers and their apparatus were destroyed by the heavy fire.

I repeatedly asked for Colonel Thorneycroft to state his view of the situation. At 1.20 p.m. I heliographed to ascertain whether Colonel Thorneycroft had assumed command, and at the same time asked General Coke to give me his views on the situation on Spion Kop. Still getting no reply, I asked whether General Coke was there, and subsequently received his view of the situation (copy attached). He stated that, unless the artillery could silence the enemy's guns, the men on the summit could not stand another complete day's shelling, and that the situation was extremely critical.

At 6.30 p.m. I asked it he could keep two battalions on the summit, removing the remainder out of reach of shells; also whether two battalions would suffice to hold the summitt. This was in accordance with a telegram on the subject sent me by the Commander-in-Chief. Later in the evening I made arrangements to send two (Naval) 12-prs, and the Mountain Battery Royal Artillery to the summit, together with half company Royal Engineers (and working parties, two reliefs of 600 men each), to strengthen the entrenchments and provide shell covers for the men. I may here mention that the 17th Company Royal Engineers proceeded at the same time as General Woodgate's force, and were employed until daylight upon the entrenchments, then upon road making and water supply.

Sandbags were sent up early on the 24th instant.

While Colonel Sim was, with this party, ascending the hill, he met Colonel Thorneycroft descending, having evacuated the position. For the remainder of the account of the proceedings I attach the reports made to me by Colonel Thorneycroft and by General Coke, together with reports on the supply of food and water rendered by Officers thus engaged. The supply of ammunition was ample.

I wish to bring to notice that I heard from all but one, expression of the admirable conduct and bravery shown by Officers and men suffering under a withering artillery fire on the summit of the slopes, and also of those who, with so much endurance, persisted in carrying up water and food and ammunition to the troops during this day.

During the day a Staff Officer of the Head-quarter Staff was present on the summit, and reported direct to the Commander-in-Chief.

At sunset I considered that the position could be held next day, provided that guns could be mounted and effective shelter provided. Both of these conditions were about to be fulfilled, as already mentioned.

In the absence of General Coke, whom I ordered to come to report in person as to the situation, the evacuation took place under orders, given upon his own responsibility, by Lieut.-Colonel Thorneycroft. This occurred in the face of the vigorous protests of General Coke's Brigade-Major, the Officer Commanding the Middlesex Regiment, and others.

It is a matter for the Commander-in-Chief to decide whether there should be an investigation into the question of the unauthorized evacuation of Spion Kop.

CHARLES WARREN, *Lieut.-General.*

Copy of a letter from General Woodgate to Sir C. Warren.

Spion Kop,

Dear Sir Charles, 24th January, 1900

We got up about 4 o'clock, and rushed the position with three men wounded.

There were some few Boers, who seemed

surprised, and bolted after firing a round or so, having one man killed. I believe there is another somewhere, but have not found him in the mist.

The latter did us well, and I pushed on a bit quicker than I perhaps should otherwise have done, lest it should lift before we get here. We have entrenched a position, and are, I hope, secure; but fog is too thick to see, so I retain Thorneycroft's men and Royal Engineers for a bit longer.

Thorneycroft's men attacked in fine style.

I had a noise made later to let you know that we had got in.

Yours, &c.,

E. WOODGATE.

Copy of letter from Lieut.-Colonel Thorneycroft to Sir C. Warren.

Spion Kop,

To Sir C. Warren.   24th January, 1900, 2.30 p.m.

Hung on till last extremity with old force. Some of Middlesex here now, and I hear Dorsets coming up, but force really inadequate to hold such a large perimeter. The enemy's guns are north-west, sweep the whole of the top of the hill. They also have guns east; cannot you bring artillery fire to bear on north-west guns? What reinforcements can you send to hold the hill to-night? We are badly in need of water. There are many killed and wounded.

ALEC. THORNEYCROFT.

If you wish to really make a certainty of hill for night, you must send more Infantry and attack enemy's guns.

Spion Kop,
24th January, 1900.

3 p.m.—I have seen the above, and have ordered the Scottish Rifles and King's Royal Rifles to reinforce. The Middlesex Regiment, Dorsetshire Regiment, and Imperial Light Infantry have also gone up, Bethune's Mounted Infantry (120 strong) also reinforce. We appear to be holding our own at present.

J. TALBOT COKE, *Major-General.*

From Colonel Thorneycroft to Chief Staff Officer to Sir Charles Warren.

24th January, 1900.

The troops which marched up here last night are quite done up—Lancashire Fusiliers, Royal Lancaster Regiment, and Thorneycroft's Mounted Infantry. They have had no water, and ammunition is running short. I consider that even with reinforcements which have arrived, that it is impossible to permanently hold this place so long as the enemy's guns can play on this hill. They have the long-range gun, three of shorter range, and one Maxim-Nordenfelt, which have swept the whole of the plateau since 8 a.m. I have not been able to ascertain the casualties, but they have been very heavy, especially in the regiments which came up last night. I request instructions as to what course I am to adopt. The enemy, at 6.30 p.m., were firing heavily from both flanks with rifles, shell, and Nordenfelt, while a heavy rifle fire is kept up in front. It is all I can do to hold my own. If casualties go on occurring at present rate I shall barely hold out the night. A large number of stretcher bearers should be sent up, and also all water possible. The situation is critical.

ALEC. THORNEYCROFT, *Lieut.-Colonel.*

Note from Colonel Thorneycroft to Sir C. Warren.

24th January, 1900.

Regret to report that I have been obliged to abandon Spion Kop, as the position became untenable. I have withdrawn the troops in regular order, and will come to report as soon as possible.

ALEC. THORNEYCROFT, *Lieut.-Colonel*

From Lieut.-Colonel A. W. Thorneycroft, Thorneycroft's Mounted Infantry, Commanding on Spion Kop, to the Chief Staff Officer to General Sir C. Warren.

Camp, Trichard's Drift,
Sir,   26th January, 1900.

On the night of the 23rd January, 1900, I rendezvoused with 18 Officers and 180 men, Thorneycroft's Mounted Infantry, 2nd Bn. Lancashire Fusiliers, 2nd Bn. Royal Lancaster Regiment, and half company Royal Engineers, the whole under the command of General Woodgate. At 9 p.m. we started to march to the top of Spion Kop. I led the way with a small advanced party, crossed the dongas and advanced up the hill; on reaching the first plateau the force closed up in formation, and went on again. As the front broadened I got the Thorneycroft's Mounted Infantry into line, right across the hill, and the remainder followed in successive lines up the last slope, when we were suddenly challenged. I had ordered the men to lie down when challenged; they did so. The Boers opened fire from magazines, when I thought that they had emptied their magazines I gave the order to charge; an Officer on my left gave the order to charge also, and the whole line advanced at the double and carried the crest line at 4 a.m., when I halted and re-formed the line. There were about 10 men wounded altogether. Orders were immediately given by General Officer Commanding to form a trench and breastwork. There was a mist on the hill, and in the darkness and mist it was difficult to get the exact crest line for a good field of fire, and the boulders made it difficult to dig, but we made a rough trench and breastwork. At 4.30 a few Boers came up and began firing. The men lined the trench, but the picquets in front replied to the fire, and firing ceased for a time. The Boers then returned with strong reinforcements from their camp, which lay concealed in a hollow on the side of the hill, and which was obscured in the mist; we sent out men in front to enable them to get a better field of fire; with two lulls in the firing, the mist rose about 8 a.m., when the rifle fire on both sides became heavy and the Boers opened fire from three guns and a Maxim-Nordenfelt. The shrapnel fire was very accurate and burst well, sweeping the whole plateau. General Woodgate was wounded early in the action and Colonel Blomfield assumed command, but he, too, was wounded. At this time I was directing the movements of the Thorneycroft's Mounted Infantry, and sent out reinforcements to the firing line which was in advance of the trench; word was sent to me that General Sir C. Warren had heliographed that I was to assume command. I sent out more men to the flanks as the Boers were working round, and the replacing of casualties gradually absorbed all the men of the force. The firing became hotter on both sides, the Boers gradually advancing; twice the men charged out from the entrenchments in the centre and kept them back, but at length the entrenchment became the firing line in the centre (the left maintained their advanced position).

The Boers closed in on the right and centre. Some men of mixed regiments at right end of trench got up and put up their hands; three or four Boers came out and signalled their comrades to advance. I was the only Officer in the trench on the left, and I got up and shouted to the leader of the Boers that I was the Commandant and that there was no surrender.

In order not to get mixed up in any discussion I called on all men to follow me, and retired to some rocks further back. The Boers opened a heavy fire on us. On reaching the rocks I saw a company of the

Middlesex Regiment advancing, I collected them up to the rocks, and ordered all to advance again. This the men did, and we reoccupied the trench and crest line in front.

As the companies of the Middlesex arrived I pushed them on to reinforce, and was able to hold the whole line again. The men on the left of our defence, who were detached at some distance from the trench, had held their ground. The Imperial Light Infantry reinforced this part. The Boers then made a desperate endeavour to shell us out of the position, and the fire caused many casualties. The Scottish Rifles came up, and I pushed them up to the right and left flanks as they arrived. There was some discussion at this time as to who was in command, and the Officer Commanding Scottish Rifles said he would go and see General Talbot Coke, who was reported to be at the foot of the hill, to get orders. Up to this I had issued the orders, but as I only got a verbal message I did not understand that I had the temporary rank of Brigadier-General. I continued to direct operations while the Officer Commanding Scottish Rifles went to see General Talbot Coke. General Coke said that Colonel Hill was in command, but I could not find him. The heavy fire continued, and the Boers brought a gun and Maxim-Nordenfelt to bear on us from the east, thus sweeping the plateau from the east, north, and north-west, and enfilading our trenches. The men held on all along the line, notwithstanding the terrific fire which was brought to bear on them, as the enemy's guns (which now numbered five and two

Nordenfelts) were absolutely unmolested. When night began to close in I determined to take some steps, and a consultation was held. The Officer Commanding Scottish Rifles and Colonel Crofton were both of opinion that the hill was untenable. I entirely agreed with their view, and so I gave the order for the troops to withdraw on to the neck and ridge where the hospital was. It was now quite dark, and we went out to warn all to come in. The enemy still kept up a dropping fire. The regiments formed up near the neck, and marched off in formation, the Scottish Rifles forming the rear guard. I was obliged, owing to want of bearers, to leave a large number of wounded on the field.

In forming my decision as to retirement I was influenced by the following:—

The superiority of the Boer artillery, inasmuch as their guns were placed in such positions as to prevent our artillery fire being brought to bear on them from the lower slopes near camp, or indeed from any other place.

By my not knowing what steps were being taken to supply me in the morning with guns, other than the mountain battery which, in my opinion, could not have lived under the long-range fire of the Boer artillery, and their close-range rifle fire.

By the total absence of water and provisions.

By the difficulty of entrenching on the top of hill, to make trench in any way cover from artillery fire with the few spades at my disposal, the ground being so full of rocks.

Finally, I did not see how the hill could be held unless the Boer artillery was silenced, and this was impossible.

Lieutenant Winston Churchill arrived when the troops had been marched off.

I have the honour to be,
Sir,
Your obedient Servant,
ALEC. THORNEYCROFT, *Lieut.-Colonel,*
Commanding Thorneycroft's Mounted Infantry.

Report of Major-General Talbot Coke, Officer Commanding 10th Brigade.
(Attack on Spion Kop, 23rd, 24th, 25th January, 1900.)

Pontoon Bridge,
25th January, 1900.

In accordance with your orders, General Woodgate assumed command of the column for the night attack, and settled his rendezvous near the Royal Engineer bivouac, for 7 p.m., 23rd instant. I bivouacked on the hill upon which the Connaught Rangers' picquets are south of Three Tree Hill.

The first shots were fired at 3.40 a.m.

The valley between my position and Spion Kop, and also the top of that feature itself, was enveloped in mist until about 8 a.m., when it could be seen that our force held the schanzes on the summit. Shortly after it was seen to be exposed to a frontal fire from rifles, and to shell fire from its left front.

In accordance with orders communicated to me by you, to send a battalion to reinforce, a signal message was sent to the Imperial Light. Infantry, which occupied a covering position towards Wright's Farm to proceed at once to support, moving by the right flank of the kop. The 2nd Bn. Dorsetshire Regiment was ordered to the place vacated by the Imperial Light Horse.

The position of Spion Kop was now seen to be exposed to a cross fire of artillery, and by your instructions I sent the Middlesex Regiment in support.

About 11.10 a.m., in consequence of the regrettable news about General Woodgate, at your order I proceeded to the kop myself. On arrival there, I found the track leading up very much congested, and, from information received, I formed the opinion that too many men were getting into the trenches and stone cover above, and becoming exposed to the artillery fire; I accordingly checked reinforcements. Soon after this, on my way up, an urgent message was received from Colonel Hill, who commanded at this time on the right, calling for reinforcements, as his line had actually fallen back before, and lost some prisoners to the Boers, who were pressing on in front. I accordingly sent up the rest of the Imperial Light Infantry available.

I now met Major Bayly, a Staff Officer, from the 4th Brigade, and he informed me that an urgent message for help had been received from Colonel Crofton, who commanded on Spion Kop, after

General Woodgate was wounded. General Lyttelton had accordingly despatched the Scottish Rifles as an actual reinforcement, and a battalion of the King's Royal Rifles against the hill to the north-west of Spion Kop. It was on the further slope of this hill that one of the Vickers-Maxim guns was placed. (This battalion worked its way some distance up the hill, but its action did not materially affect the situation.)

I now again received an urgent appeal for support, this time for the centre and left. I sent the Scottish Rifles.

I now had only as a reserve Bethune's Mounted Infantry and the Dorsetshire Regiment. These I retained and they were not engaged at the actual front.

The shell fire was most galling, and was aimed not only at the summit, but at the crest of the spur leading up, along which reinforcements and parties bringing back wounded had to pass. The fire came—

1. From field guns firing shrapnel and common shell, situated, as I endeavoured to point out in a signal message to you, north-west of our position.

2. From a Vickers-Maxim, in about the same direction.

3. From a similar gun to the north-east.

All these were beyond the effective rifle fire, and our supporting Artillery on and about Three Tree Hill and on the Dragoon's Maxim position apparently could not see them, consequently they poured, unchecked, an uninterrupted cross fire on to our position from about 8 a.m. till dark—10 hours.

Losses were very heavy, owing to the numbers

necessarily assembled to hold back the Boer frontal attack, established under cover, and in which they showed gallantry in pushing forward to our lines. Colonel Crofton was now reported wounded, and the command of the troops in front devolved on Colonel Hill, Commanding 10th Brigade.

So the situation continued until 6 p.m., when I wrote a report and despatched it to you by Colonel Morris, A.A.G. (I request that this document, to save labour, may be attached). I first showed this to Colonel Hill, and he concurred, even taking exception to my reference to a retirement. I had no doubt that the Infantry, which had so gallantly held its own all day, would be able to continue to do so when the shell fire abated at nightfall.

I accordingly went back to my reserves, having personally handed over command at the summit to Colonel Hill.

About 9.30 p.m., in consequence of your orders, I left for your camp, leaving a Staff Officer (Captain Phillips) behind. The narrative must now be his

About 11.30 p.m. this Officer, who was sleeping, was awakened by the sound of men moving, and found a general retirement proceeding.

He allowed no one to pass after this, stopped the Scottish Rifles, and collected a large number of stragglers of the Dorset, Middlesex, and Imperial Light Infantry. Bethune's Mounted Infantry and the bulk of the Dorsets remained in position as posted in support to the front line. The other corps had gone down the hill.

He then published memorandum (v), attached, to all companies, except Lieut.-Colonel Thorneycroft, who had gone on; but they did not act upon it, urging that they had had distinct orders from Lieut.-Colonel Thorneycroft, who, as far as I knew, was only assisting Colonel Crofton in a portion of the front line, to retire.

We now held the spur to within about 300 yards of the summit, but the summit itself was evacuated. Signal communication could not be established at the moment, as the lamp which the signalling Officer counted upon ran out of oil, and some time was lost in obtaining another.

About 1.30 a.m. a person, not by his speech an Englishman, was brought in on suspicion by a picquet. He made a statement to the effect that a Naval gun would shertly be brought up, and requested that it might not be fired on. This was the first intimation of any Naval gun coming to Spion Kop.

About 2.20 a.m. a Naval Officer reported that he had one 12-pr. gun below Spion Kop, near the donga on the west. He said he had orders to take this up to the summit. When asked whether he could do so before daylight, he said he could not. As it would be impossible to move the gun in any line after daybreak, on account of hostile fire, he was told to stand by in a place of safety. Signalling communication was now opened, and the attached message (vi) sent.

As Captain Phillips got no instructions, about 2.30 a.m. he ordered vehicles back to place of safety.

All regimental wagons had been sent across by the Deputy-Assistant Ajutant-General (B), 5th Division.

Shortly after 4 a.m., there still being no orders, and a mass of transport, small-arm ammunition carts, &c., at the donga, steps were taken to cover this passage, and, with the concurrence of the Officer Commanding Dorsetshire Regiment, and Officer Commanding Scottish Rifles, certain dispositions were made with the latter battalion and about half the former. The other half of the Dorsetshire Regiment were employed in carrying away a large number of boxes (about 80) of small-arm ammunition, brought back from the front and elsewhere.

The Imperial Light Infantry, Middlesex, and Thorneycroft's had apparently gone home. Bethune's were dismissed.

It was now light, and Boer "sniping" commenced. Captain Phillips reported to me at the donga, about 4.45 a.m., when I was in possession of your order as to the pontoon crossing.

> TALBOT COKE, *Major-General,*
> *Commanding Right Attack.*

(i.)

Officer Commanding 10th Brigade, or any Officer,
    Clear out left flank.

> W. J. BONUS, *Brigade-Major*

(ii.)

There are enough on the kopje, direct the others round the sides of the hill, 3.45 we hope to charge, at any rate at nightfall.

> W. J. BONUS.

(iii.)

To General Talbot Coke, 24th January, 1900, 5.5 p.m.

We have now plenty of men for firing line, but the artillery fire from our left (west) is very harassing, I propose holding out till dark and then entrenching.

AUG. W. HILL, *Lieut.-Colonel.*

(iv.)

Officer Commanding Imperial Light Infantry,

Withdraw, and at once. 2 a.m.

W. J. BONUS, *Brigade-Major*

(v.)

Officers Commanding Dorsetshire and Middlesex Regiments,

Scottish Rifles, Imperial Light Horse.

This withdrawal is absolutely without the authority of either Major-General Coke or Sir Charles Warren.

The former was called away by the latter a little before 10 a.m.

When General Coke left the front about 6 p.m. our men were holding their own, and he left the situation as such, and reported that he could hold on.

Someone, without authority, has given orders to withdraw, and has incurred a grave responsibility. Were the General here, he would order an instant reoccupation of the heights.

H. E. PHILLIPS,
Deputy-Assistant Adjutant-General.

(vi.)

Spion Kop, 25th January, 1900, 2.30 a.m.
General Officer Commanding Three Tree Hill,

Summit of Spion Kop evacuated by our troops, which still hold lower slopes. An unauthorized retirement took place.

Naval guns cannot reach summit before daylight; would be exposed to fire if attempted to do so by day.

PHILLIPS.

(vii.)

Regimental Transport Officers, 25th January, 1900, 2.30 a.m.

All vehicles should be withdrawn to a place of safety, either towards Wright's Farm, or up the gully across the drift.

By order

D. PHILLIPS.

Extract from Commanding Royal Engineer's Diary, 5th Division, 24th January.

Hatting's Spruit, 28th January, 1900.

About 3 a.m. (Commanding Royal Engineer, 5th Division) I was ordered by General Officer Commanding to take the second half company of the 17th Company Royal Engineers to Spion Kop, to make zigzag roads up the steepest parts for mules to take up water and the Mountain Battery.

The half company, under Captain Hedley, R.E., and with Lieutenant Neill, R.E., crossed the valley, and started work at dawn from the bottom of the slopes. I went to the top with Captain Hedley to choose out the best places, and on arrival we found the first half company, under Major Massey, R.E., had almost completed their intrenching work, and he sent back all but a sub-section to assist in the road making. As the party was collecting tools and falling in, though the hilltop was in a thick cloud, the enemy opened musketry fire, and all troops took cover; the fire was not replied to and ceased after about 10 minutes. I then took the Royal Engineer party down. I also found water from small springs about halfway up the hill, and some men were set to collect it on the side of the hill that was not exposed to fire. Broad slides were also made down some of the boulder slopes up which guns might be dragged by hand. I returned to camp at 10.30 a.m.

At 10.30 Captain Buckland, R.E., was sent to 17th Company to get sandbags taken to the hill. These (about 2,000) were taken by a small cart to the drift, and thence a rear company of a battalion going across (Dorsetshire Regiment), and the company native drivers of 17th Company Royal Engineers, carried about 1,000 up the hill, the remainder were left as a reserve at the drift to be taken up later. Captain Buckland returned to camp about 12.

At 12.30 Captain Buckland went to Venter's Spruit to procure three coils of 3-inch cable from 17th Company wagon, to enable the Naval guns to be hauled up the hill at night. This was deposited at 17th Company camp about 2.30, to be ready for the guns when passing that way.

About 5 p.m. General Officer Commanding showed me a letter from Sir R. Buller, of which the following is an extract:—

"If you send up either mountain guns or 12-pr. they should make some very strong epaulments, 8 feet thick, covering the gun from the line of its extreme fire, thus—

"If this is done, any gun to attack it must come in front of it."

General Officer Commanding ordered me to be ready to do this, and also to take working parties at night to deepen the trenches on Spion Kop, so that they might screen the defenders from shell fire, being made 4 feet deep and sloping backwards inside, in the same form as the Boer "schanzes" are made.

I arranged with Officer Commanding 17th Company for the tools and for the half company that was now on Spion Kop to remain there, so that the Officers and non-commissioned officers might super-intend the working parties. At 9 p.m. General Officer Commanding ordered me to proceed and make epaulments for two Naval guns (12-pr.), each to be 23 feet diameter, and to give 4 feet 3 inches cover; also epaulments as above for the Mountain Battery, and to improve the trenches. He gave me also a letter to Colonel Thorneycroft, urging him to hold the hill, and explaining the work I had been ordered to do. To carry the tools across a party of 200 Somersetshire Light Infantry was detailed, and two reliefs, of 600 each, for the work were to be drawn from the reserve battalions on Spion Kop rear slopes.

About 12 p.m., when I (with Captain Buckland, R.E.) had led the tool-carrying party about quarter the way up the slopes of Spion Kop, we met Colonel Thorneycroft coming down, having ordered a retirement. I gave him General Officer Commanding's letter, and he said it was too late, as the men, unsupported by guns, could not stay. He ordered me to take my party back. I sent them back with Captain Buckland, and then went forward to ascertain if the retirement was general. Finding it so, I walked up the valley to warn the Officer in command of the Naval gun of the altered situation, and prevent him risking his gun by moving it to the evacuated hill top.

The 37th Company Royal Engineers had been telegraphed for from Spearman's about 4 p.m. It started at once, and arrived at the 17th Company camp about 1.30 a.m. (25th). It then moved off with tools for Spion Kop, but was met by Captain Buckland, R.E., who informed the Officer Commanding of the retirement. After proceeding a short distance, Major Cairnes, R.E., Commanding, halted, and sent Captain Harper to the hill for information and orders. I found the company on my return about 2.30 a.m., and ordered it to bivouac where it was, and await further orders.

J. H. SIM, *Lieut.-Colonel, R.E.,*
Commanding Royal Engineer, 5th Division.

From Major H.N. Sargent, D.A.A.G. (B), 5th Division, to General Officer Commanding, 5th Division.

Sir,   28th January, 1900.

With regard to the water supply on Spion Kop, I have the honour to report that the arrangements made were as follows:—

All the available pack mules which could be procured—viz., 25—were utilized in carrying biscuit tins, filled with water, up the hill, the tins being refilled from water carts placed at the foot of Spion Kop. Each tin contained 8_ to 9 gallons of water. An Officer was placed in charge of the water carts, and had a plentiful supply of spare tins, in addition to those carried by the mules. The mules were divided into two sections, each under an Officer. These two sections of mules conveyed to the troops up the hill at each trip 425 gallons of water.

The water supply was kept going continuously during the day and late at night, with the exception of one break, caused by an order being given for one section of mules to bring up ammunition. In addition to the water conveyed on mules, there was a spring at the top of the hill, under Royal Engineer charge, which yielded a fair supply. I superintended generally the water supply myself, and made frequent enquiries as to whether the troops were getting sufficient quantity on top of the hill, and was told they were. A little delay was occasioned in the early part of the morning in looking for packalls, which I was told were in the camp, but which could not be obtained.

With regard to the food supplies, as soon as ever the drift near Spion Kop was made passable for our wagons, I collected the regimental wagons at the foot of the hill and instructed the regimental officers in charge to communicate with their units as to getting the supplies up the hill, which was done, and the boxes of biscuit and meat were taken up by hand.

I have the honour to be,

Sir,

Your obedient Servant,

H. N. SARGENT, *Major,*

D.A.A.G. (B).

From Major E. J. Williams, D.A.A.G., to the General Officer Commanding, 5th Division.

Springfield Camp,

Sir,   28th January, 1900.

I have the honour to report for your information that, on the 24th January, I undertook to take water to the troops engaged at Spion Kop Hill. I guided 12 mules loaded with water to the trees near the top of the hill, arriving there about 12 noon. It was my intention to take the water to the field hospital on the top, but just as I arrived it was destroyed by shell fire, and the Medical Officer requested me to deposit the water where it was. The mules then made a second trip, and a water depôt was established. After this all mules were seized to convey ammunition to the firing line. The Royal Engineer company dug for water, which was found three-quarters of the way up the hill; it was thick, but fairly plentiful. At 3 p.m. I impressed some more mules, and from that time to 8 p.m. I continued to hurry up water to the water depôt; also men were sent up with filled water bottles for distribution to the firing line. At 8 p.m. it was too dark for the mules to work, and although several fell over the cliff in getting up, there were at this hour several full boxes of water at different spots on the hill.

Supplies of all kinds were plentiful at the foot of the hill, and in conjunction with the water, I impressed all mules, horses, and straggling men to carry up rations before darkness came on, but it is impossible to say if these actually reached the front line, as it was impossible to see what was going on, owing to the troops going up and the stretcher bearers coming down.

I have the honour to be,

    Sir,

        Your most obedient Servant,

            E. J. WILLIAMS, *Major,*

            D.A.A.G.

From Colonel A. W. Morris, A.A.G., 5th Division, to General Officer Commanding, 5th Division.

28th January, 1900.

Re the water supply on Spion Kop, I beg to report as follows:—

I accompanied General Coke up Spion Kop, about 11 a.m., 24th instant. About half way up the hill, just by the trees on the Kop, we came across a depôt water supply, under a non-commissioned officer; I should say there were some 20 tins of water under this non-commissioned officer's charge. Numbers of men asked this non-commissioned officer for water, but he said it was reserved for the wounded. On this General Coke ordered a certain number of tins to be placed aside for the unwounded men, this the non-commissioned officer did at once; I think he set aside for the unwounded about five tins. No doubt many of the tins under his charge were empty, but I cannot say, as I was anxious to get further up the hill. However, when I got further up the hill, I saw several men bringing up by hand tins of water to the firing line. When I arrived at the firing line mules, loaded with ammunition, came up, and the General ordered the ammunition to be unloaded, and the mules sent back to the water supply depôt to bring up more water tins. Whether these ever arrived I cannot say, as I shortly afterwards went down the hill to carry a letter to the General Officer Commanding, 5th Division.

Personally, I do not think the men were suffering very badly from want of water. I consider that, under the circumstances, nothing could have been better than the very difficult arrangements made for water supply; it was not plentiful, but sufficient for the purpose required.

A. W. MORRIS, *Colonel,*
A.A.G., 5th Division.

From Field-Marshal Lord Roberts to the Secretary of State for War.

Army Head-quarters, South Africa,
My Lord   Camp Jacobsdal, 17th February, 1900.

In continuation of my letter, dated 13th February, 1900, I have the honour to forward the enclosed telegram from General Sir Redvers Buller, requesting that certain words may be inserted in his despatch describing the operations at Spion Kop.

I have the honour to be,

My Lord,

Your Lordship's most obedient Servant,

ROBERTS, *Field-Marshal,*

Commander-in-Chief, South Africa.

From the General Commanding-in-Chief, Natal, to the Military Secretary, Cape Town.

Spearman's Camp,
31st January, 1900, 1.20 a.m.

I posted my report on operations, 7th to 30th January, yesterday, when you receive it, will you please insert after the words "enclose his report of his oper-ations," the following words:—

"As Sir Charles Warren does not allude to it, I may mention that on the 21st reinforced him by the 10th Brigade, made up to four complete battalions by the addition to it of the 2nd Bn. Somersetshire Light Infantry and the Imperial Light Infantry, a local corps 1,000 strong, for whose services he particularly asked."—BULLER.

From General Sir Redvers Buller to the Secretary of State for War

Secretary of State   2nd February, 1900.

I forward this. It is certain that General Warren did receive the message in the terms he quoted, I saw it myself, and he also repeated it to General Lyttelton, who has quoted it in his report. The signal station was not in or very near the firing line.

I have an impression that the message referred to by Lieutenant Martin was sent as well as that quoted by General Warren, but I have not been able to verify this idea.

One thing is quite clear, about the time this message was sent one portion of the front line did propose to surrender, and it was Colonel Thorneycroft, and not Colonel Crofton, who refused the surrender and rallied the men.

REDVERS BULLER,
General Officer Commanding.

Chief of Staff,   Hatting's Farm, 1st February, 1900.

With reference to my despatch on the "capture and evacuation of Spion Kop" already sent to you, I have now to forward a statement made by Colonel Crofton, Commanding 2nd Bn. Royal Lancaster Regiment, regarding the message which was signalled to me from the summit of Spion Kop, and which (as I have already reported) reached me in these words: "Reinforce at once, or all lost. General dead."

It seems certain that no message was written down at the transmitting station on Spion Kop, and the only written record is that of the message received at the receiving station with me.

C. WARREN, *Lieut.-General,*
Commanding 5th Division.

From Colonel Crofton, Commanding 2nd Bn. Royal Lancaster Regiment, to the Brigade-Major, 11th Brigade.

Sir,   Hatting's Farm, 31st January, 1900.

I beg most strongly to protest against the message reputed to be sent by me from Spion Kop on the 24th, stating "All is lost." Such a message was never sent by me, nor did it ever enter my thoughts to send such a message, as the circumstances did not call for it. My message given to the Signalling Officer (Lieutenant Martin, Royal Lancaster Regiment) was: "General Woodgate dead; reinforcements urgently required." This I considered necessary, as the Boers were increasing in numbers every minute, and I had no means of ascertaining the numbers of the reserves that they had to draw upon.

I very much feared some error had occurred from the returned message, directing me under no circumstances to surrender, and I felt most deeply being superseded during the engagement by an Officer so very much my junior.

I have the honour to be,
    Sir,
        Your most obedient Servant,
        MALBY CROFTON, Colonel,
          Royal Lancaster Regiment.

Hatting's Farm,
31st January, 1900.

Officer Commanding Lancaster Regiment,

It would strengthen your case if you attached the message handed to Lieutenant Martin for despatch, and also call upon the signallers who signalled the message wrongly sent in your name to account for having despatched a message not properly authenticated by signature.

A. WYNNE, A.A.G.,
Commanding 11th Brigade.

Brigade-Major   31st January, 1900.

Lieutenant Martin's statement herewith.

MALBY CROFTON, *Colonel.*

31st January, 1900.

Lieutenant Martin, Signalling Officer

Be good enough to let me have a full report hereon of the message I gave you to send from Spion Kop on the 24th, relative to General Woodgate's reported death, and asking for reinforcements.

MALBY CROFTON, *Colonel.*

To Colonel Crofton, Commanding 2nd Bn. Royal Lancaster Regiment.

Hatting's Farm,
Sir,   31st January, 1900.

On 24th instant, soon after firing began, I was looking for some signallers, you met me, and said, "I must have a signaller;" I said, "I am looking for them."

You replied: "Get them at once, and send a message to Sir Charles Warren and say General Woodgate is dead, and ask for reinforcements at once."

I called for signallers, and two men of 2nd Bn. Lancashire Fusiliers ran up. We went to a spot that I selected, and found that there was already a signaller there, Private Goodyear, of the West Yorkshire Regiment (he was with Lieutenant Doomer, R.A., observing the effect of artillery fire).

I said to Private Goodyear, "You might send a message for me whilst the helio is being put up."

I told him to call up "G.O.C." the station I wished to communicate with, and to say, "General Woodgate is killed; send reinforcements at once." I did not write the message down, as I had no paper.

I have the honour to be,

Sir,

Your obedient Servant,

A. R. MARTIN, *Lieutenant,*
2nd Bn. Royal Lancaster Regiment.

Hatting's Farm,
A A.G., 5th Division   31st January, 1900.

Forwarded. It is unfortunate that the message was not written. I believe the order is that signallers should not accept any message that is not written and signed.

A. WYNNE, *Major-General,*
Commanding 11th Brigade.

V

From the General Commanding-in-Chief, Natal, to the Secretary of State for War
(By the Field-Marshal Commander-in-Chief, Cape Town.)

Spearman's Hill Camp,

Sir, 30th January, 1900.

I have the honour to forward to you the enclosed reports relative to recent operations in the vicinity of the River Tugela:—

I ordered these operations to be undertaken on the eastern line, in order to free me as much as possible whilst operating on the western line.

I also forward a report from Major-General the Hon. N. G. Lyttelton, on the action taken by him during the operations of 24th January, but this should be read in connection with Sir C. Warren's of that day.

I have the honour to be,

Sir,

Your obedient Servant,
REDVERS BULLER, *General*.

The Brigade Major, Fusilier Brigade,

Chieveley Camp,
Chieveley,   19th January, 1900.

With reference to this day's operations towards Robinson's Drift, as the Mounted Infantry under my command got into difficulties down by the river, I beg to report, for the information of the General Officer Commanding, my orders to that unit.

Lieutenant Renton, two other Officers, and 40 non-commissioned officers and men reported themselves to me at 5 a.m. here. I told Lieutenant Renton, who had been out towards the drift with the General Officer Commanding and myself the previous evening, that I was going to move down with my Infantry and guns towards the drift, and that I wanted him to cover my advance and protect my flanks with his Mounted Infantry. I said, "Information is what I want, as I can tackle the enemy should they come on." I told him I should like one Officer and 15 men for each flank, and that 10 men would do very well for the front; on this he went away, and sent his men out. I told him my formation with Infantry and guns, and where I should be; I received no reports from him, but some two hours after, when I eventually arrived with my extended line on a ridge of hills overlooking the river and Robinson's Drift, some 3,200 yards from it, I met Lieutenant Renton, who reported to me that the enemy were not our side of the river, and that one or more of his men had been down to the drift and said it was unfordable. I then told him I much wanted to know for certain about the drift, and anything that could be seen of the enemy or their defences the other side, and suggested a place for a cossack post, where his men would be under cover and out of sight, and to try from there to get the information, but I repeated several times, "I do not want your men to get fired upon." Lieutenant Renton went down to this place, reported it suitable, and posted his men. About that time I got the report of 1,000 of enemy on my left flank, which caused me to send Lieutenant Renton off to his men on that flank, and myself to watch it and give sundry orders; this report turned out to be false, and during this time we had seen the Boers moving down the hill the other side of the river and occupy different places. It was then that I found out that there were several Mounted Infantry scouts with their horses along the river in my front; they were, I believe, some of the 10 men who had covered my front in the morning, extended to some 200 yards, had gone down to the river and remained there; the Boers having come down towards the river they were in a very awkward position, as they could not withdraw without being under Boer fire. The difficulty was to extricate the men, I ordered up the two Mountain Battery guns and got them into action, and also requested the Naval guns to shell a certain donga, which they did; further, my machine guns got into action, and tried some long-range volleys. The two latter methods were no good, but under cover of the guns several were got away; eventually, Lieutenant Renton reported to me that he had, as far as he could make out, four of five men away and three horses, I left Lieutenant Renton and a sufficient force of Mounted Infantry to watch for his men, as I expected they would get away when the Boers retired back from the river or else under cover of darkness. I never gave Lieutenant Renton to understand he had to hold the river line or seize the drift; 10 men would not have been much good for such an undertaking. The cossack post from which I thought he could have reconnoitred the drift should, in my opinion, have been done by one or two men dismounted.

I commend the pluck of the men who came back from the river, two of them under a very hot fire. One man on foot made his way back across the open, and Lieutenant Jones, of the 8th Hussars, galloped down, picked him up, and brought him in on his horse, a plucky action, though, as it happened, he was not

hotly fired on. Further, two men on the right, galloping on their horses, fell; one was left without a horse,
and appeared to be wounded. Captain and Adjutant
Braithwaite at once galloped out and picked the man
up; he had damaged his foot, but had not been shot.

C. THOROLD, *Lieut.-Colonel,*
Commanding 1st Bn. Royal Welsh Fusiliers.
Camp, Chieveley,

Chief of Staff,   20th January, 1900.

Transmitted. I have communicated the same to
General   Officer   Commanding   Lines   of
Communication, Maritzburg.

I very much regret these most unnecessary casualties. It was distinctly explained to Captain Renton,
and by him to his men, that they were going out to
reconnoitre, not to fight.

It was not necessary for the scouts to go right
down to the river bank, as a bare ridge overlooks the
river at about 1,000 yards from the bank.

Having reached the river bank, however, the
scouts should have withdrawn to high ground, as
Colonel Thorold thought they had done. I have carefully questioned the serjeant who was in command of
the scouts in front, and he says that five or six of his
men dismounted on the bank and took good cover.
He went along the river to examine the drift, and
after a long time the Boers opened fire, and he
shouted out to retire, and he and four of his men galloped back, being hotly fired upon. Two of the men
led their horses wounded, and returning on foot, were

helped back by two mounted Officers. The remaining men apparently kept under cover, and lost their opportunity of retiring.

After the force had withdrawn, three Boers were seen to leave the trenches and go down to the bank, and the six men, South African Light Horse, were seen all together, and taking off their coats on the south bank. Shortly after, nine or ten men were seen on north bank moving away from the river towards the hills. It is concluded our men waded across and surrendered, and they were not wounded.

G. BARTON, *Major-General,*
Commanding at Chieveley.

REPORT of Action near Potgieter's, 20th January, 1900.

Sir,   Camp over Potgieter's Drift.

Having received a telegram from Lieut.-General Sir C. Warren early in the morning of the 20th instant, that he was attacking the enemy north of Fair View, and that a demonstration by me against the Boer position opposite the drift might create a useful diversion, I ordered the 3rd Bn. King's Royal Rifles to advance and occupy some small kopjes on the left and a farmhouse on the right, about midway between my position and the Boers. This was accordingly done at about 10 a.m., and the balloon was also sent forward, in order to get a nearer and a better view. There was a donga to the right front of the farmhouse, about 300 yards in advance, which was occupied by one company, Captain Beaumont's. This company immediately came under a sharp fire at comparatively short range, and the party in the farmhouse were also fired on to a lesser degree. For some hours the damage done was quite trifling, one man only had been hit by 3 p.m.; but later on, one if not two machine guns were brought up, and casualties began to occur. It was very difficult to say from whence the fire came until the machine guns opened, probably from small parties concealed behind rocks and banks. To relieve the former, fire was opened by two Naval 12-prs. and two howitzers, assisted by the two 4.7-inch guns, and at about 5 p.m. the 64th Field Battery moved out and opened fire at about 2,400 yards from the Boers. The fire appeared singularly effective, searching the hillsides thoroughly, and the Boers were seen bolting in every direction from the shells. Their fire was promptly silenced, and there is good reason to believe that two machine guns were knocked out. As usual, it is impossible to say what loss the Boers suffered, but judging from their inability to face the shell fire and the accuracy of our fire, there must have been some; moreover, an ambulance was seen moving along the position. At 5.30 p.m. the 2nd Bn. Scottish Rifles and the 1st Bn. Rifle Brigade moved out covered by artillery fire, and the whole force eventually withdrew under cover of night. I should add that the force on the left was also fired upon, but only one or two men were hit. It is hoped that the demonstration had some effect in forcing the enemy to their trenches, and preventing them from assisting the force fighting Sir C.

Warren, which was the object aimed at. The King's Royal Rifles had a long and trying day, and I was quite satisfied with their behaviour.

The balloon was hit by a bullet, and Captain Phillips, R.E., also had a narrow escape while in the air. Useful work in investigating the Boer position and in directing our fire was done by the balloon Officers.

I have the honour to be,

Sir,

Your obedient Servant,

N. G. LYTTELTON, *Major-General,*
Commanding 4th Infantry Brigade.

From Officer Commanding Bethune's Mounted Infantry to Brigade-Major, 4th Brigade.

Potgieter's Drift,
21st January, 1900.

I moved out yesterday with two squadrons of my regiment in the direction of Swartz Kop, and skirmished towards the hills on the east of the enemy's position, opposite Swartz Kop. We drew the enemy's fire, and made them expose themselves. There were about 300 to 400 men on the hill. We killed one Boer and wounded one horse. Ammunition expended, 325 rounds. No casualties on our side. Returned to camp 7.15 p.m.

The squadron that went over Wagon Drift reports that a heavy engagement was going on. A shell burst among them, killing one horse and wounding two others. Three rifles were lost by this squadron while crossing the river. I have ordered a Court of Enquiry to enquire into the matter.

E. BETHUNE, *Lieut.-Colonel,*
Commanding Bethune's Mounted Infantry
Chieveley,

Chief of Staff,   23rd January, 1900.

Such persistent reports have reached the Intelligence Department at Head-quarters, from various sources, regarding the Boers having left Cingol, Hlangwani, and even Colenso, that I determined to clear up the matter to-day by a reconnaissance in such force as I could muster. For this purpose (as I have only two battalions here) Colonel Blagrove brought from Frere 120 mounted men and two guns, and 400 men of the Rifle battalion, who were railed over.

I moved two guns (Naval 12-prs.) to the advanced gun position west of railway, escorted by 300 Riflemen; left flank covered by 50 South African Light Horse.

Colonel Blagrove, with 170 mounted men and two field guns, moved to Hussar Hill to reconnoitre. I supported him with 10 companies of Royal Fusiliers and Royal Welsh Fusiliers, and two Naval 12-prs., which I moved forward far enough to the right front to shell Hlangwani and the Boer camp between Nât Hill and Bloy's Farm.

Work was continuing in the trenches about Colenso, and these were shelled.

A pont and ferry boat were discovered above

Colenso road bridge,and a landing stage; Boers were seen to cross to the south side, and they were shelled with effect.

Colonel Blagrove reconnoitred from the right in a masterly manner, and located a considerable number of Boers, who opposed him in trenches, which were peppered effectually by the field guns.

Unfortunately, a young Officer of Bethune's Mounted Infantry, while reconnoitring, got 10 men into a stone kraal, and they were being surrounded when Colonel Blagrove succeeded in extricating the Officer and seven men. Three appear to have been captured, as they are missing. The Boers showed considerable determination, and followed up the mounted men when withdrawing, but I was able to check their offensive movement by shell fire from the 12-prs., which were ably handled by Lieutenant Richards, R.N. It is estimated that from 300 to 500 actually opposed Colonel Blagrove; his entire force was under a heavy fire, and there is no doubt the position is still strongly held by the Boers.

I saw numbers of Boers about the trenches at Fort Wylie and kopjes near there, but I did not take my Infantry within rifle range of the river.

My Cavalry scouts were fired at from Colenso, and from the river bank above Colenso.

The Boers' train steamed rapidly out of Colenso, and the 12-prs. failed to hit it.

My casualties will be reported later. They are, I believe, four men missing, five wounded, including Captain de Rougemont, South African Light Horse, severely wounded, and not yet brought to camp, but an ambulance has gone to fetch him.

The Cingol camp is still occupied, and supplied to-day two Boer contingents to reinforce the Hlangwani force.

G. BARTON, *Major-General,*
Commanding at Chieveley.

P.S.—During the day the Boers did not reply with a gun, but, according to information of my scouts, there is still one on Hlangwani, and several at Colenso, the latter probably of no great value.

G.B.

From Officer Commanding Troops, Frere, to Chief of Staff.

Frere,
Sir,   24th January, 1900.

I have the honour to inform you that, on the 23rd instant, I co-operated with Major-General Barton in a demonstration in front of Colenso, with troops from Frere, as per margin.

Under instructions from General Barton, I recon-noitred with the mounted troops, viâ Hussar Hill, towards Hlangwani Mountain.

Having cleared the ridges in front by scouts of the South African Light Horse and Bethune's Mounted Infantry, the guns came into action on Hussar Ridge, and shelled the trenches on Hlangwani and slopes to the south-east, supported by a half squadron 14th Hussars. At the same time the South African Light

Horse, Bethune's Mounted Infantry, and Mounted Infantry 4th and 5th Brigades, advanced and reconnoitred the enemy's position. The latter came on in considerable force, and after closely reconnoitring the enemy's position, the Colonial troops and Mounted Infantry were compelled to fall back, and I retired on Chieveley. The reconnaissance was completely successful in compelling the enemy to disclose their positions, and showed that Hlangwani Mountain is held in considerable strength. A small party of Bethune's Mounted Infantry was for a time isolated in a kraal somewhat far advanced, and in covering their retirement, casualties occurred.

I regret to say that Captain de Rougemont, of the South African Light Horse, from Chieveley, was dangerously wounded and is since dead. Captain Dalton, R.A.M.C., proceeded, in the most gallant manner to his assistance, but was severely wounded whilst attending him.

I have the honour to be,

Sir,

Your obedient Servant,

H. BLAGROVE, *Lieut.-Colonel,*
Commanding Troops, Frere.

Camp, Potgieter's,

Chief of Staff,   25th January, 1900.

I have the honour to report as follows:—

On my return from the kopjes at 10 a.m., I received a telegram from Sir C. Warren, marked A. This appeared to be so urgent that I ordered two squadrons of Bethune's Mounted Infantry, the Scottish Rifles, and the King's Royal Rifles, to cross at the Kaffir Drift, under Naval Gun Plateau, with these orders, the two first to join Sir C. Warren's extreme right and place themselves under the orders of the General Officer Commanding at that point. Message B was received at 10.15 a.m. The first corps crossed—Bethune's at 11.45 a.m., Scottish Rifles, 12.30 p.m., and King's Royal Rifles at 1 p.m. As the first parties were crossing, I noticed that strong reinforcements were reaching Sir C. Warren's right, which was unduly crowded with troops. It seemed unnecessary to send more men then, and with a view of creating a diversion, I directed Colonel Riddell to move his battalion against Sugar Loaf Hill, and the hill between it and the right of the main position. I had misgivings that there was too wide an interval, and in instructing Colonel Ridd-II verbally, I told him to use extreme caution, sending out scouts and only extending two companies, and having a half battalion in reserve. I told him I could not give him definite instructions, and must leave a good deal to his discretion. At about 2.30 p.m. I received message C from Major Bayly, and at once ordered, by signal, the Officer Commanding King's Royal Rifles to retire slowly until further orders. See message D. This order was again repeated by signal at 3.30 p.m. (message E), and by mounted orderly at 4.50 p.m. (message F). Considerable delay appears to have occurred before any of these were received, the hills being some distance in rear of the battalion, and it was not till 5 p.m.

that I received helio message G. At 5.15 p.m. I saw that a portion of the battalion had reached the top of the hill, and at 6 p.m. I received flag message H from Officer Commanding who was at top of Sugar Loaf. At 6 p.m. I sent message K by mounted orderly, ordering him to retire under cover of darkness, which was done without loss; I had no idea that the battalion was anywhere near the top of the hill. The advance was wonderfully well carried out, and the ascent of the precipitous hillside was a very fine feat, of which the battalion may be justly proud. I greatly regret the losses incurred, but I do not think they were fruitless. I have learnt that the men on Sir C. Warren's right say that without this diversion they could not have held their position, and I have heard from Sir C. Warren (message L) that my assistance had been most valuable.

I have the honour to be,
   Sir,
      Your obedient Servant,
         N. G. LYTTELTON, *Major-General,*
         Commanding 4th Infantry Brigade.

COPIES OF Telegrams, &c., of 24th January, 1900.

A.—From Sir Charles Warren to General Lyttelton. (Received 24th January, 1900, 10 a.m.)
   "Give every assistance you can on your side. This side is clear, but the enemy are too strong on your side, and Crofton telegraphs that if assistance is not given at once all is lost. I am sending up two

battalions, but they will take some time to get up."

B.—From some person unknown to General Lyttelton. (Received 24th January, 1900, 10.15 a.m.)

"We occupy all the crest on top of hill, being heavily attacked from your side. Help us. Spion Kop."

C.—From Major Bayly, Staff Officer to General Lyttelton. (Received 24th January, 1900, 2.30 p.m.)

"Very hot fire here, near flag, which is our observing station; only just holding our own. Bethune's and Scottish Rifles are now coming up. Do not think that King's Royal Rifles can get up on right; it is held by Boers. We are only holding up to your left of saddle. A heavy fire from Boers on our north-west, where they have a gun, which is causing damage. Cannot see left of our line or the Boers. Water badly wanted."

D.—From Brigade-Major, 4th Brigade, to Officer Commanding King's Royal Rifles (by heliograph). (Sent 24th January, 1900, 3 p.m.)

"Retire steadily until further orders."

E.—From Brigade-Major, 4th Brigade, to Officer Commanding King's Royal Rifles (by heliograph). (Sent 24th January, 1900, 3.30 p.m.)

"Retire steadily till further orders. Please say how last message was transmitted."

F.—From Brigade-Major, 4th Brigade, to Officer Commanding King's Royal Rifles (by mounted orderly). (Sent 24th January, 1900, 4.50 p.m.)

"No. 141. Unless the enemy has retired you will fall back, under cover of darkness, to the bridge just made, which is near the ford you crossed at, and where a fire will be lit, after dark, to guide you. Keep this orderly if of any use. Manners is at ford, with stretcher bearers, if you want any. Hope all is well."

G.—From Officer Commanding King's Royal Rifles to Brigade-Major (by heliograph). (Received 24th January, 1900, 5 p.m.)

"If I can recall the advanced sections I will do so, but it is difficult to communicate, and the hill is fearfully steep. I have two or three wounded to help down."

H.—From Officer Commanding King's Royal Rifles to Brigade-Major (by flag). (Received 24th January, 1900, 6 p.m.)

"We are on top of the hill. Unless I get orders to retire I shall stay here."

J.—From Brigade-Major to Officer Commanding King's Royal Rifles (by flag). (Received 24th January, 1900, 6 p.m.)

"Retire when dark."

K.—From Brigade-Major to Officer Commanding King's Royal Rifles (by mounted orderly). (Sent 24th January, 1900, 6 p.m.)

"No. 144. I am sending you a signal lamp. The General Officer Commanding considers you could not hold the Sugar Loaf unsupported, and having no troops to support you with, he orders a retirement across the foot-bridge below ford, and bivouac on Naval Gun Plateau. Please report when you get in. I have rum, tea, and wood ready for you."

L.—From General Warren to General Lyttelton (by wire). (Received 24th January, 1900, 6.50 p.m.)

"The assistance you are giving most valuable. We shall try to remain in statu quo during to-morrow. Balloon would be of incalculable value."

From the General Officer Commanding, Natal, to the Secretary of State for War.

(By the Field-Marshal Commanding-in-Chief, Cape Town.)

Spearman's Hill Camp,

Sir, 30th January, 1900.

In continuation of my letter of this date, I have the honour to enclose two additional reports from Major-General Barton, as under:—

Report dated 24th January, relative to the action of a party of the enemy in firing upon and severely wounding Captain Dalton, R.A.M.C., whilst attending to a wounded Officer.

Report dated 25th January, relative to the same, and to the death of Captain de Rougemont, South African Light Horse.

This is a regrettable circumstance. As a rule the enemy treat our wounded with great kindness.

I have the honour to be,

   Sir,

     Your obedient Servant,

      REDVERS BULLER, *General*.

            Camp, Chieveley,

        Head-quarters,24th January, 1900.

The Chief of the Staff,

I have the honour to make the following report for information of the General Commanding in Natal.

I have just seen Surgeon-Captain Dalton, R.A.M.C., who was brought in wounded this morning, and he made the following statement to me, viz.:—

"I was out with a squadron of the 14th Hussars yesterday, and during the engagement near Hlangwani, Lieut.-Colonel Blagrove pointed to a man on the ground, and said, 'There's a wounded man. ' I went across and found an Officer of the South African Light Horse, and four men of the Mounted Infantry, who had carried the wounded officer to the spot for safety from fire. I dismounted, and was attending to the wounded Officer, when some Boers rode up from the flank to within about 100 yards. I gave my white handkerchief to one of the men, and told him to wave it, which he did. I told another to take the Geneva Cross armlet off my arm and hold it up, which he did. In spite of this, they opened fire and shot two of us, myself and one of the men."

Apart from the signals made, there cannot possibly have been any shadow of doubt as to the meaning of the little group of men, kneeling and bending over the prostrate form of the dangerously wounded Officer.

I fear that Captain Dalton's wound is very dangerous, as he was struck in the abdomen. He is a fine and gallant Officer, wearing, besides war decorations, the medal of the Royal Humane Society.

I refrain from making any comment on the dastardly conduct of the Boers on this occasion.

I have the honour to be,

Sir,

Your obedient Servant,

G. BARTON, *Major-General,*

Commanding at Chiereley.

Chief of the Staff,   Chieveley, 25th January, 1900.

In continuation of my letter of the 23rd instant, I regret that my casualties on that date amounted to one Officer and three men killed, one Officer and five men wounded, and 12 men missing,.

It appears that as the Officer of Bethune's Mounted Infantry (Lieutenant Coke) had returned from the kraal referred to in my letter, Colonel Blagrove had been informed that the Officer and seven men had escaped. This, however, was not the case, as 11 of Bethune's Mounted Infantry are missing, and were no doubt taken prisoners.

As regards the other casualties, Captain Dalton's condition being more favourable, I again questioned him as to what occurred when he was wounded, and he has supplied the following further information:—

"When the Boers fired upon the party attending to Captain de Rougemont, it appears that of the four men who had carried that Officer away, one was killed, two were wounded, and one was taken prisoner. When the Boers came up to them, they took from the men's pockets all they required and went away. Of the two wounded men, one afterwards died."

Owing to the above circumstance, I deeply regret to say that Captain de Rougemont was not found until the following morning.

Captain Dalton, however, said that the wound was very dangerous, and the case hopeless from the first, and it appears that the deceased Officer became delirious soon after he was wounded, and remained so until he died in the ambulance on his way to camp.

The Medical Officers with lanterns were searching the ground until a late hour on the 23rd to find Captain de Rougemont, not knowing that all his attendants were hors de combat.

I have the honour to be, Sir,

Your obedient Servant,

G. BARTON, *Major-General,*

VI

From Lieut.-General Sir George White. V.C., G.C.B., G.C.S.I., G.C.I.E., late Commanding the Ladysmith Garrison, to the Chief of the Staff to the Field-Marshal Commanding-in-Chief in South Africa.

Cape Town,

Sir,   23rd March, 1900.

In my despatch dated 2nd December, 1899, addressed to the Secretary of State for War, and forwarded through you, I brought down the history of events relating to the force under my command to the evening of 30th October, 1899. On the morning of the following day, General the Right Honourable Sir Redvers Buller, V.C., G.C.B., K.C.M.G., arrived at Cape Town and assumed command of the whole of the forces in South Africa. On the 10th January, 1900, Field-Marshal Lord Roberts took over the chief command. I have now the honour to report, for his Lordship's information, the events which have taken place from that date until the 1st March, 1900, on which day Sir Redvers Buller arrived in Ladysmith, having successfully carried out the relief of this long besieged town.

It will be remembered that during October, 1899, the forces of the Orange Free State and the South African Republic had been gradually converging on Ladysmith from west and north, and that, although my troops had successfully encountered portions of the enemy's armies at Talana, Elandslaagte, and Rietfontein, the battle of Lombard's Kop on 30th October had proved that the numbers and mobility of the Boer forces, when once concentrated, were too great to admit of any prospect of victory should I continue with inferior numbers to oppose them in the open field. The task before me was the protection from invasion by the Boers of as large a portion as possible of the Colony of Natal, and especially of Pietermaritzburg, the capital of that Colony and the seat of its Government; and I had now to consider how this could be best insured. On 31st October General Sir Redvers Buller telegraphed to me as follows:—"Can you not entrench and await events, if not at Ladysmith then behind the Tugela at Colenso?" On the same date I replied, stating my intention to hold on to Ladysmith, and on 1st November I received Sir Redvers Buller's approval of this course in a telegram which commenced as follows:—"I agree that you do best to remain at Ladysmith, though Colenso and line of Tugela river look tempting."

It may be well to state here shortly the reasons which governed my choice of this position. Ladysmith is the most important town in Northern Natal, and there was reason to believe that the enemy attached very great and perhaps even undue importance to obtaining possession of it. It was suspected then, and the suspicion has since been confirmed that the occupation of that town by the Boer forces had been decided on by the disloyal Dutch in both Colonies as the signal for a general rising; as, in fact, a material guarantee that the power of the combined Republics was really capable of dealing with any force the British Empire was able to place in the field against them. Our withdrawal would, therefore, have brought about an insurrection so widespread as to have very materially increased our difficulties. Strategically the town was important as being the junction of the railways which enter Natal from the Transvaal and the Orange Free State, and until the Republics could gain possession of that junction their necessarily divergent lines of supply and communication prevented their enjoying to the full the advantages of combined action. Tactically the place was already partially prepared for defence and offered a natural position of some strength; and although the perimeter which must be occupied was very great for the number of troops available, yet it afforded a possibility of maintaining a protracted defence against superior numbers. On the other hand, the mere fact of a retirement behind the Tugela would have had a moral effect at least equal to a serious defeat, and would have involved the abandonment to the enemy of a large town full of an English population, men, women, and children; and of a mass of stores and munitions of war which had been already collected there before my arrival in South Africa, and had since been increased.

The line of the Tugela from the Drakensberg to the Buffalo River is some 80 miles long, and in a dry season, such as last November, can be crossed on foot almost anywhere. Against an enemy with more than double my numbers, and three times my mobility, I could not hope to maintain such a line with my small force, and any attempt to prevent their turning my flanks could only have resulted in such a weakening of my centre as would have led to its being pierced. Once my flank was turned on the line of the river the enemy would have been nearer Maritzburg than I should have been, and a rapid withdrawal by rail for the defence of the capital would have been inevitable. Even there it would have been impossible to make a prolonged defence without leaving it open to the enemy to occupy the important port of Durban, through which alone supplies and reinforcements could arrive, and for the defence of which another retreat would have become eventually essential; thus abandoning to the enemy the whole Colony of Natal from Lang's Nek to the sea. On the other hand, I was confident of holding out at Ladysmith as long as might be necessary, and I saw clearly that so long as I maintained myself there I could occupy the great mass of the Boer armies, and prevent them sending more than small flying columns south of the Tugela, which the British and Colonial forces in my rear, aided by such reinforcements as might be shortly expected, could deal with without much difficulty. Accordingly, I turned my whole attention to preparing Ladysmith to stand a prolonged siege.

With this object in view, I employed my troops during 31st October and 1st November in improving and strengthening the defences of the various positions surrounding Ladysmith, which together enclosed the area which I had determined to hold. During these days the Boers gradually pushed round from north and west to the south and east of the town, which underwent a slight bombardment on 1st November. On 31st October, General Koch, of the Army of the South African Republic, who had been wounded and taken prisoner at Elandslaagte, died, and his widow was permitted to remove his body for burial in the Transvaal. Before leaving she expressed her gratitude for the courtesy and kind treatment which both her late husband and herself had received at our hands. On the same date I despatched the 2nd Bn.

Royal Dublin Fusiliers and Natal Field Battery by rail to Colenso to assist in the defence of the bridges over the Tugela. During the night of 1st-2nd November, the Boers brought several new guns into position, and although the Naval Brigade, under Captain the Hon. H. Lambton, R.N., opened fire from one of the naval 4.7-inch guns on the morning of 2nd November, the bombardment of the town became much more severe than on the previous days. At about 4 a.m., the 5th Dragoon Guards, 5th Lancers, 18th Hussars, Natal Mounted Volunteers, and 69th Battery, Royal Field Artillery, moved out south into the Long Valley to reconnoitre the enemy and to endeavour to surprise one of his camps in the direction of Onderbook. Major-General French, who was in command, left Colonel Royston with the Natal Mounted Volunteers and two guns to hold the Nek between Wagon Hill and Middle Hill, and with the remainder of his force passed round the southern end of End Hill (where he left a squadron of the 5th Lancers to hold a ridge, dismounted), and gaining the plateau pushed on about 3,000 yards and opened an effective fire on the Boer camp. The enemy evacuated their camp and took up a position on a ridge to which they brought up field guns. Major-General French, having fulfilled his mission, withdrew his force, reaching camp by 10 a.m. Our casualties were one man wounded.

As he returned to Ladysmith a telegram was received from General Sir Redvers Buller, desiring that Major-General French and his staff might be sent to the Cape. Communication by wire and rail were still open, and although trains were constantly fired upon, advantage had been taken of the fact to send southward as many of the civil population of Ladysmith as were willing to depart. Major-General French and his staff left by train about noon on 2nd November, and a telegraphic report was received here that although the train had been heavily fired on near Pieter's Station, it had reached Colenso in safety. Immediately afterwards the wires were cut by the enemy, and railway communication was interrupted. Ladysmith was thus isolated from the world outside it, and from this date the siege may be held to have commenced.

On 3rd November, four squadrons, Imperial Light Horse, under Major Karri Davies, who were reconnoitring to the south, found a body of the enemy, with one gun, on Lancer's Hill, and asked for reinforcements to drive them off. The 5th Dragoon Guards, 18th Hussars, 19th Hussars, and 21st Battery, Royal Field Artillery (the whole under Brigadier-General J. F. Brocklehurst, M.V.O.), were accordingly sent down the Long Valley to their assistance. The 19th Hussars seized Rifleman's Ridge and endeavoured to turn the enemy's left, while the 18th Hussars covered the right rear; two companies of Infantry, detached from Cæsar's Camp, occupied Wagon Hill, and a Mounted Infantry company seized Mounted Infantry Hill to protect the left rear; while the 5th Dragoon Guards and 21st Field Battery were moved straight down the Long Valley. Meantime two squadrons, Imperial Light Horse, were holding

Middle Hill, while the remaining two squadrons were facing the enemy on Lancer's Hill. The squadrons on Middle Hill were opposed to a considerable body of the enemy, who were moving up from the east. The 21st Field Battery opened fire on Lancer's Hill and quickly silenced the enemy's gun. Believing that the enemy were evacuating the hill the two squadrons, Imperial Light Horse, made a gallant but somewhat ill-advised attempt to occupy it, but though they seized and held a portion of the hill the enemy was in too great strength for further progress. In the meanwhile I had sent out the Natal Mounted Volunteers and the 42nd and 53rd Field Batteries to join Brigadier-General Brocklehurst, and to cover his retirement, if necessary. General Brocklehurst sent the Natal Mounted Volunteers to reinforce the Imperial Light Horse squadrons on Middle Hill, and brought both batteries into action in the Long Valley. Finding, however, that the numbers of the enemy in his front and on both flanks were continually increasing, and that he could not hope to press his reconnaissance further without serious loss, he determined to withdraw. With the assistance of a dismounted squadron, 5th Dragoon Guards, under Major Gore, the squadrons, Imperial Light Horse, on Lancer's Hill were retired under cover of Artillery fire till they reached the main body, when the whole force engaged was gradually withdrawn to camp. Our loss was two Officers and two non-commissioned officers and men killed. Three Officers and 23 non-commissioned officers and men wounded, and one man missing. The enemy's loss is reported to have been considerable, chiefly from our Artillery fire.

In the afternoon the enemy made demonstrations of an attack in force on Devonshire Post, which was reinforced as a measure of precaution, but the attack was not seriously pressed, and was repulsed with ease. The bombardment this day was very heavy, a large number of shells falling into the town, and especially in and around the hospitals, which were in various churches and public buildings near the centre of the town. In the evening a deputation of civilian residents of Ladysmith waited on me with the request that permission might be obtained for them to pass through the enemy's lines and proceed to the south. The Principal Medical Officer of the Force also represented that the effect of the bombardment on the large number of wounded in his hospitals was very bad, and asked that, if possible, an agreement might be arrived at for the hospitals to be placed outside the town. Next morning I sent Major Bateson, R.A.M.C., under flag of truce, with a letter to General Joubert, asking that these requests might be agreed to on grounds of humanity to sick, wounded, and non-combatants. In reply, General Joubert agreed to my hospitals being moved out of Ladysmith to a point on the flats, 4 miles down the railway and close to the Intombi Spruit. He refused to allow the civil inhabitants to go south, but permitted them to accompany the sick and wounded to the Intombi Camp. Food and all other requisites for this camp were to be supplied from Ladysmith, and, for this purpose, one train was to be allowed to run each way daily, and by daylight only, under flag of truce. On the same day General Joubert sent into Ladysmith six Officers of the Royal Army Medical Corps, 10 Assistant Surgeons, and 98 of our wounded from Dundee; together with a number of Indian hospital attendants. There was a threatening of attack on Cæsar's Camp on this night, 4th November, but it was not pressed. Our first communications by pigeon post to Durban were sent off on this date.

5th November was Sunday. Throughout the siege Sundays have generally been observed by both sides, as far as possible, as days of rest from fighting. There has been no special arrangement on the subject, but a kind of tacit understanding came into existence that neither side would fire unless specially provoked to do so by the construction of fortifications or other signs of movement on the opposite side. 5th November was no exception to this rule, and advantage was taken of the day to send our sick and wounded and all such civilians, men, women, and children, as elected to go, to the Intombi Camp.

The defences of Ladysmith were, for the purposes of command, divided into four sections, "A," "B," "C" and "D." "A" section, under Colonel W. G. Knox, C.B., commenced at Devonshire Post and extended to the point where the Newcastle Road passes between Junction Hill and Gordon Hill. "B" section included all the defences from Gordon Hill round to Flagstone Spruit, and was commanded by Major-General F. Howard, C.B., C.M.G., A.D.C. "C" section under Colonel Ian Hamilton, C.B., D.S.O., comprised the ground from Flagstone Spruit to the eastern extremity of Cæsar's Camp. "D" section, under Colonel Royston, Commandant of the Natal Mounted Volunteers, included the thorn country north of Cæsar's camp and the Klip River Flats. The troops, which were allotted to these sections, and to the general reserve, and the variations in these arrangements which were, from time to time, found necessary.

On 6th November, 2nd Lieutenant R. G. Hooper, 5th Lancers, reached Ladysmith with despatches. Arriving in Natal too late to join his regiment before communication was cut off, he most gallantly made his way through the Boer lines at night, and on foot, accompanied only by a Kaffir guide.

All the provisions in the shops and stores in the town were taken over on this date and administered as part of the general stock, all civil residents being placed on rations which were issued free or on payment according to their means.

Next day, 7th November, Cæsar's Camp was subjected to a heavy fire of shells and long range musketry. Although no actual attack was made, it was found advisable to send the Imperial Light Horse to reinforce this point; while the 42nd Battery, Royal Field Artillery, under Major Goulburn, was placed in position on the plateau during the night, the horses returning to camp. A number of natives of India were sent into Ladysmith by the Boers.

On 8th November a 6-inch gun opened fire from the top of the Bulwana Mountain. Throughout the siege this gun has proved most trouble-some to the defence. On the same day a number of refugees from Dundee, both English and Indian, were sent into Ladysmith by the Boers, and were located by us in the Intombi Camp.

. 9th November was ushered in by a very heavy fire at dawn on all sides of our defences from the enemy's artillery, which included several new guns, which now opened for the first time, and whose exact positions it was very hard to locate. This was followed by a general advance of their infantry and the devel-opment of a severe musketry action at Cæsar's Camp, in the thorn bush north of that ridge, at Devonshire Post and Observation Hill. The steady front shown by our troops prevented the enemy from trying to close, and although on Cæsar's Camp, where the 1st Bn. Manchester Regiment, under Lieut.-Colonel A. E. R. Curran, rendered very valuable service, the action lasted until darkness set in, yet elsewhere it had mostly died away at 12 noon. At that hour I proceeded, with my Staff, to the Naval Battery on Gordon Hill, whence a salute of 21 shotted guns, in honour of the birthday of the Prince of Wales, was fired at the enemy by Captain the Hon. H. Lambton, R.N., and three cheers were given for His Royal Highness, which were taken up by the troops both in camp and on the defences. A message of congratulation, to be telegraphed to His Royal Highness, was despatched by pigeon post to Durban. Our casualties during the day amounted to 4 men killed, 4 Officers and 23 men wounded. It is difficult to form any accurate estimate of the enemy's losses, but they certainly considerable exceeded our own.

From 10th to 13th November, inclusive, very little of importance occurred, the fire both of guns and rifles being much less severe than usual. An Irish deserter from the Boers gave himself up on the 12th November. From him we learnt that the total force then surrounding us here numbered about 25,000 men, that they were mounting more guns, and expected to be reinforced shortly.

On 14th November, I sent Brigadier-General J. F. Brocklehurst, M.V.O., with two regiments of Cavalry, two batteries of Artillery and detachments of the Imperial Light Horse and Natal Mounted Volunteers, across the Klip River, to try and work out on one or both sides of Rifleman's Ridge into the more open country beyond, to find out the enemy's strength in that direction, and, if possible, to capture one of their wagon convoys, of which several had recently been seen passing at a distance of some miles. The Natal Mounted Volunteers and Imperial Light Horse seized Star Hill, but after shelling Rifleman's Ridge for some time General Brocklehurst decided that it was too strongly held for him to leave it in his rear, while an attempt to storm it would have been more costly than the occasion would justify. He, therefore, returned to camp. On this night the Boers commenced for the first time to shell the town and camps at night, opening fire from their heavy guns about midnight for a few minutes, a practice which they maintained nightly for about a week, and then discontinued.

From this time nothing worth record took place until 19th November, when the Boers sent into Intombi Camp six privates of the 2nd Bn. Royal Dublin Fusiliers, who had been wounded in the attack on an armoured train near Colenso, on 15th November.

20th November was marked by an unusual number of casualties from shell fire, chiefly among the 18th Hussars and Gordon Highlanders.

Next day General S. Burger sent in a letter under a flag of truce, complaining that we had been running trains at night to the Intombi Camp, contrary to our agreement with General Joubert—a complaint for which there was no foundation whatever. He also inquired why a Red Cross flag was flying on the Town Hall although our hospital was at Intombi. I replied, on 22nd November, by giving my personal assurance that trains never had been and never would be, run to Intombi at night, and explaining that the Red Cross flag was hoisted on the Town Hall because that building was in use as a hospital for ordinary cases of sickness, and for slightly wounded men whom it was not worth while to send to Intombi. Before my answer could reach him the Boer guns were deliberately turned on the Town Hall, which was several times struck.

On 23rd November the enemy endeavoured, under flag of truce, to send into Ladysmith 230 Indian coolies. It became evident that the intention was to send in here as many non-combatants as could be collected who would be useless for defence, but would help to consume our supplies. For this reason I refused to receive them, and requested that they might be sent to the Officer commanding our forces south of the Tugela. I understand that this course was eventually adopted. Copies of the correspondence are attached . The same evening an attempt was made to wreck the only engine which the enemy possessed on the Harrismith line. With this object an old locomotive was selected from those in the railway yard here and was sent off down the line, at night, with a full head of steam and with the safety valve screwed down. The Boers had, however, provided against such an attempt by destroying a culvert on our side of their temporary terminus, and here our engine was derailed and upset. The enemy evidently feared that it carried a cargo of explosives, as they did not approach it next morning until they had sent a number of shells into it from their artillery.

On the 24th November we had the misfortune to lose 228 oxen, which were captured by the enemy. Owing to lack of rain the grazing within our lines had become insufficient for all our animals, and a number of our cattle had to be grazed outside our defences, wherever a re-entrant gave them some protection from capture. Owing to the carelessness of certain civilian conductors, these oxen were allowed to stray too far out and seeing this the Boers commenced bursting shells on our side of the cattle in order to hasten their movements. In this they were

successful, the Kafirs in charge abandoning their animals in order to seek shelter. As soon as the
occurrence was noticed, the Mounted Infantry
Company of the 1st Bn. Leicestershire Regiment,
under Captain C. Sherer, was sent out to try and head
them back, but it was then too late, and though
Captain Sherer did all that was possible and drove
back a considerable number, under a heavy musketry
fire from the enemy, yet, as already mentioned, the
enemy obtained possession of 228 head.

Beyond the usual daily bombardment, nothing
worth recording took place till 27th November,
which was marked by the unmasking of a new 6-inch
gun on Middle Hill, and a very evident increase in the
number of Boers in our immediate vicinity. An attack
on our positions seemed likely, and all precautions
were taken accordingly, but next day news arrived of
Major-General Hildyard's fight at Mooi River, and
the consequent withdrawal of the Boers to the north
of the Tugela, which fully explained the increased
numbers visible from Ladysmith.

On the 28th November, two 6.3-inch howitzers
were sent to occupy emplacements which had been
prepared for them on the reverse slope of Wagon Hill;
a naval 12-pr. was also placed on Cæsar's Camp. From
this position they opened fire next day, and proved
able to quite keep down the fire from the enemy's 6-
inch gun on Middle Hill, which some days afterwards
was withdrawn from that position. I arranged an
attack on Rifleman's Ridge for the night of 29th
November, but was compelled to abandon it, as just at

sunset the enemy very strongly reinforced that portion of their line. There can, I think, be no doubt that my plan had been disclosed to them, and indeed throughout the siege I have been much handicapped by the fact that every movement, or preparation for movement which has taken place in Ladysmith, has been at once communicated to the Boers. The agents through, whom news reached them, I have, unfortunately, failed to discover. I have sent away or locked up every person against whom reasonable grounds of suspicion could be alleged, but without the slightest effect.

Two civilians, who had volunteered to blow up the Sunday's River railway bridge, started on their perilous journey on 29th November, and returned here on 1st December. They reached the bridge without mishap, and duly placed the charges, but owing to not fully understanding the use of the fuse, only one out of four charges exploded.

On 29th November also we observed flashing signals on the clouds at night from Estcourt and were able to read a portion of a message. At a later period of the siege no difficulty was experienced in reading such messages, but we were without the means of replying in similar fashion.

30th November was a day of very heavy bombardment, a new 6-inch gun opening fire from Gun Hill and doing much damage. One shell in particular entered the Town Hall which we had hitherto used as a hospital, killing and wounding 10 persons. It was found necessary to evacuate the building and place the hospital under canvas in a gorge where the protection from shell fire was better. This severe bombardment continued throughout 1st and 2nd December, but fortunately proved comparatively harmless. On the latter date heliographic communication viâ Weenen was restored after having been interrupted for a long period.

On 3rd December General Joubert sent me a letter alleging that we had made unfair use of the Intombi Camp, and proposing that it should be broken up. In reply, I dealt in detail with the points raised, none of which had any foundation in fact, and as a result the breaking up of the camp was not pressed.

On 5th December, at 1.30 a.m., two companies of the 2nd Bn. Rifle Brigade moved out, under Captain J. E. Gough, to surprise Thornhill's Farm which the enemy were in the habit of occupying with a picket at night. The enterprise was very well conducted, but the farm was unfortunately found unoccupied.

On the night of 7th December, Major-General Sir A. Hunter, K.C.B., D.S.O., made a sortie for the purpose of destroying the Boer guns on Gun Hill, which had been giving us much annoyance. His force consisted of 500 Natal Volunteers, under Colonel Royston, and 100 men Imperial Light Horse, under Lieut.-Colonel A. H. M. Edwards, with 18 men of the Corps of Guides, under Major D. Henderson, D.A.A.G. for Intelligence, to direct the column, and four men Royal Engineers and 10 men No. 10

Mountain Battery, Royal Garrison Artillery, under Captain Fowke and Lieutenant Turner, Royal Engineers, with explosives and sledge hammers for the destruction of the guns when captured. Sir A. Hunter's arrangements were excellent throughout, and he was most gallantly supported by all his small force. Gun Hill was taken, a 6-inch Creusot and a 4.7-inch howitzer destroyed, and a Maxim captured and brought into camp. Our loss was only one Officer and seven men wounded. I consider that Major-General Sir A. Hunter deserves the greatest credit for this very valuable service for which he volunteered. He brings to my notice specially the gallant behaviour of Colonel W. Royston, Commanding Volunteers, Natal, Lieut.-Colonel A. H. M. Edwards (5th Dragoon Guards), Commanding Imperial Light Horse, Major D. Henderson, D.A.A.G. for Intelligence (wounded), Major A. J. King, Royal Lancaster Regiment, Major Karri Davis, Imperial Light Horse, Captain G. H. Fowke, R.E., and Lieutenant E. V. Turner, R.E., whose names I have much pleasure in bringing forward for favourable consideration.

The same night three companies of the 1st Bn. Liverpool Regiment, under Lieut.-Colonel L. S. Mellor, seized Limit Hill, and through the gap in the enemy's outpost line thus created, a squadron 19th Hussars penetrated some 4 miles towards the north, destroying the enemy's telegraph line and burning various kraals and shelters ordinarily occupied by them. No loss was incurred in this enterprise. At the same time five companies 1st Bn. Leicestershire Regiment, under Lieut.-Colonel G. D. Carleton, visited Hyde's and McPherson's farms, usually occupied by the enemy as night outposts, but found them evacuated.

The slight opposition met with by these various operations of the night of 7th-8th December made it appear probable that the enemy had unduly weakened his force to the north of us in order to strengthen that opposing Sir Redvers Buller on the Tugela. Recognising that if this proved to be the case there might be an opportunity for my Cavalry to get far enough north to damage the enemy's railway, I ordered Brigadier-General J. F. Brocklehurst, M.V.O., to move out at dawn with 5th Lancers, 5th Dragoon Guards, and 18th Hussars and 53rd Battery, Royal Field Artillery, along the Newcastle Road, to feel for the enemy and discover his strength and dispositions. The reconnaissance was carried out in a very bold and dashing manner by the 5th Lancers and 18th Hussars, the 5th Dragoon Guards being in reserve. The enemy, however, proved to be in considerable strength, and having obtained the information I required I directed Brigadier-General Brocklehurst to withdraw his brigade. The effect of these various enterprises was shortly evident in the return from the line of the Tugela next day of some 2,000 Boers.

On the 10th December, Lieut.-Colonel C. T. E. Metcalfe, Commanding 2nd Bn. Rifle Brigade, volunteered to carry out a night enterprise against a 4.7-inch howitzer on Surprise Hill. The undertaking was one of very considerable risk, as to reach that hill it was necessary to pass between Thornhill's and Bell's Kopjes, both of which were held by the enemy. Lieut.-Colonel Metcalfe moved off about 10 p.m., with 12 Officers and 488 men of his battalion, together with a destruction party under Lieutenant Digby Jones, R.E., and succeeded in effecting a complete surprise, his advance not being discovered until he was within 4 or 5 yards of the crest line, which was at once carried, and the howitzer destroyed. The retirement, however, proved more difficult, since the enemy from Bell's and Thornhill's Kopjes, consisting apparently of men of various nationalities, closed in from both sides to bar the retreat. Lieut.-Colonel Metcalfe, however, fixed bayonets, and the companies, admirably handled by their captains, fought their way back to the railway line, where a portion of the force had been left in support, and from which point the retirement became easy. A number of the enemy were killed with the bayonet, and his total casualties must have been very considerable. Our own loss amounted to 1 Officer and 16 men killed, 3 Officers and 37 men wounded, and 6 men missing. The affair reflects great credit on Lieut.-Colonel C. T. E. Metcalfe and his battalion, and I have much pleasure in bringing to your notice, in a subsequent portion of this despatch, the names of the Officers who particularly distinguished themselves on this occasion.

My attention was now chiefly directed to preparations for moving out a flying column to co-operate with General Sir Redvers Buller. All these preparations, including the movement of a 4.7-inch and a 12-pr. gun, both belonging to the Royal Navy, were completed by 15th December. Meanwhile the enemy had moved his 6-inch gun from Middle Hill to Telegraph Hill, and on 12th December I moved down the 6.3-inch howitzers to near Ration Post to oppose it.

The firing of Sir Redvers Buller's guns from the direction of Colenso had been audible for some days, and was especially heavy on 15th December. On 16th, Sir Redvers heliographed that he had attacked Colenso on the previous day, but without success. Although this news was naturally disappointing to the hopes of immediate relief which they had entertained, yet it was received by both soldiers and civilians without any discouragement, and with a cheerful readiness to wait until the necessary reinforcements should arrive. From this time up to the close of the year few other events of importance occurred, but on Christmas day a telegram was received from Her Majesty and most gratefully appreciated by the garrison of Ladysmith. At this period a few of the many shells daily fired into our camps were especially destructive, one shell, on the 18th December, killed and wounded 10 men and 12 horses of the Natal Volunteers. Another, on 22nd December: killed 8 and wounded 9 of the Gloucestershire Regiment; and, on the same day a single shell wounded 5 Officers and the serjeant-major of the 5th Lancers. On 27th December, again, one shell killed 1 Officer of the Devonshire Regiment and wounded 8 Officers and 1 private of that regiment. During this period, also, fresh complaints regarding the Intombi Camp were made by the enemy; and, by agreement with General S. Burger, Major-General Sir A. Hunter was sent to that camp to hold an enquiry. A few minor irregularities were discovered and corrected, and a copy of Sir A. Hunter's report was sent to General Burger, who was apparently satisfied that the complaints were without serious foundation.

At the close of the year my chief source of anxiety lay in the heavy and continuous increase in the number of the sick, which had risen from 475 on 30th November to 874 on 15th December, and to 1,558 on the last day of the year. Enteric fever and dysentery were chiefly responsible for this increase, there being 452 cases of the former, and 376 of the latter under treatment on 31st December.

The Boers opened the new year by a fire of heavy guns at midnight, but beyond the daily long-range bombardment, nothing of importance occurred until 5th January, when we shelled, by indirect fire, two Boer camps, one behind Bell's Kopje, and one near Table Hill on the Colenso Plateau. In the latter case the fire probably had little effect, as the range was too great even for the naval gun employed, and the only possible observing station was very inconveniently placed. It was subsequently ascertained from the Boers themselves that the shells falling into the camp behind Bell's Kopje had been very effective, stampeding the horses and compelling the enemy temporarily to vacate the camp and seek shelter elsewhere.

On the 6th January the enemy made a most

determined but fortunately unsuccessful attempt to carry Ladysmith by storm. Almost every part of my position was more or less heavily assailed, but the brunt of the attack fell upon Cæsar's Camp and Wagon Hill. On the night of the 5th-6th January, Cæsar's Camp was held by its usual garrison, consisting of the 1st Bn. Manchester Regiment; the 42nd Battery, Royal Field Artillery; a detachment of the Royal Navy; with a 12-pr. gun; and a detachment, Natal Naval Volunteers. Wagon Hill was held as usual by three companies, 1st Bn. King's Royal Rifle Corps, and a squadron, Imperial Light Horse. A detachment, Natal Naval Volunteers, with a 3-pr. Hotchkiss gun, had been sent there on the evening of the 5th January, and two naval guns, one a 4.7-inch and the other a 12-pr., were in process of transfer to the hill during the night. These guns were accompanied by naval detachments and a working party of Royal Engineers and Gordon Highlanders, who were consequently on Wagon Hill when the attack commenced at 2.30 a.m. on the morning of 6th January. This attack was first directed on the centre of the southern face of Wagon Hill, whence it spread east and west. It fell directly on the squadron of Imperial Light Horse, under Lieutenant G. M. Mathias, and the Volunteer Hotchkiss Detachment, under Lieutenant E. N. W. Walker, who clung most gallantly to their positions, and did invaluable service in holding in check till daylight the Boers who had gained a footing on the hill within a few yards of them. The extreme southwest point of the hill was similarly held by a small mixed party of Bluejackets, Royal Engineers, Gordon Highlanders, and Imperial Light Horse, under Lieutenant Digby Jones, R.E. The remainder of the hill was defended by the companies of 1st Bn. King's Royal Rifle Corps. Shortly after 3 a.m. an attack was developed against the south-east end of Cæsar's Camp (which was garrisoned by the 1st Bn. Manchester Regiment), and on the thorn jungle between that Hill and the Klip River, which was held by the Natal Mounted Volunteers. As soon as the alarm reached me, I ordered the Imperial Light Horse, under Lieut.-Colonel A. H. M. Edwards, to proceed as rapidly as possible to Wagon Hill, and the Gordon Highlanders to Cæsar's Camp. Shortly afterwards, four companies, 1st Bn. King's Royal Rifle Corps, and four companies, 2nd Bn. King's Royal Rifle Corps, were ordered to march at once on Wagon Hill, and the 2nd Bn. Rifle Brigade on Cæsar's Camp. This section of my defences was under the command of Colonel Ian Hamilton, C.B., D.S.O., who, judging that Wagon Hill was the point most seriously threatened, proceeded there himself, where he arrived about dawn, bringing with him a company of the 2nd Bn. Gordon Highlanders under Major Miller Wallnutt. Perceiving that the close and deadly nature of the fighting made it impossible for one Officer to adequately command on both hills, I directed Colonel Hamilton to devote his attention to Wagon Hill, while I entrusted the defence of Cæsar's Camp to Lieut.-Colonel A. E. R. Curran, 1st Bn. Manchester Regiment, who had been stationed there with his battalion ever since the commencement of the siege, and was specially acquainted with the locality. I ordered Major W. E. Blewitt's battery of Royal Field Artillery, escorted by the 5th Dragoon Guards, to move out by Range Post and endeavour to prevent reinforcements reaching the enemy from the west. Major A. J. Abdy's battery of Royal Field Artillery I sent to Colonel Royston, Commanding Natal Mounted Volunteers, to take up position on the Klip River flats and shell the south-eastern corner of Cæsar's Camp, where the enemy had effected a lodgment.

The Imperial Light Horse reached Wagon Hill at 5.10 a.m., and were at once pushed into action. They pressed forward up to and over the western edge of the flat crest of the hill to within a few yards of the enemy, who held the opposite edge of the crest. They thus afforded a most welcome relief to the small garrison of the hill, but they themselves suffered very severely in occupying and maintaining their position. The company of 2nd Bn. Gordon Highlanders, which arrived with Colonel Hamilton, was sent under cover of the western slopes to reinforce the extreme south-west point of the hill, and to endeavour to work round so as to outflank the enemy, but were unable to do so owing to the extreme severity of the fire kept up by the Boers from Mounted Infantry Hill and from every available scrap of cover in Bester's Valley, which they occupied in great numbers. At 7 a.m., four companies 1st Bn. King's Royal Rifle Corps and four companies 2nd Bn. King's Royal Rifle Corps arrived, and about 8 a.m., one of these companies, followed shortly afterwards by another, was sent to reinforce the extreme south-western point of the hill, but although gallantly holding their own under a rain of shells and bullets, no progress could be made either there or on the main ridge. Meanwhile the 21st and 42nd Batteries, Royal Field Artillery, and the naval 12-pr. on Cæsar's Camp, were in action against Mounted Infantry Hill and the scrub on either side of it, and were of great assistance in keeping down the violence of the enemy's fire. Colonel Hamilton, seeing plainly that the only way of clearing out those of the enemy's marksmen who were established on the eastern crest of Wagon Hill, within a few yards of our men, was by a sudden rush across the open, directed Major Campbell to tell off a company of the 2nd Bn. King's Royal Rifle Corps to make the attempt, which how-ever failed, Lieutenant N. M. Tod, who commanded, being killed, and the men falling back to the cover of the rocks from behind which they had started. The fighting continuing stationary and indecisive, at 10 a.m. I sent the 5th Lancers to Cæsar's Camp and the 18th Hussars to Wagon Hill, two squadrons 19th Hussars having been previously posted on the ground near Maiden Castle to guard against any attempt of the enemy to turn Wagon Hill from the west.

For some time the fighting slackened consider-ably, the Boers being gradually driven down below the crest line, except at a single point where they were favoured by excellent cover, with a flat open space in front of it. At 1 p.m., however, a fresh assault was made with great suddenness on the extreme south-west point of the hill, our men giving way for a moment before the sudden outburst of fire and retiring down the opposite slope. Fortunately the Boers did not immediately occupy the crest, and this gave time for Major Miller Wallnutt, 2nd Bn. Gordon Highlanders, Lieutenant Digby Jones, R.E., Lieutenant P. D. Fitzgerald (11th Hussars), Adjutant Imperial Light Horse, Gunner W. Sims, R.N., and several non-commissioned officers, Imperial Light Horse, to rally the men; while Major E. C. Knox, Commanding 18th Hussars, brought up a portion of his regiment, which was in reserve at the foot of the hill, to act dismounted.

The top was reoccupied just as the three foremost Boers reached it, the leader being shot by Lieutenant Digby Jones, R.E., and the two others by No. 459 Trooper H. Albrecht, Imperial Light Horse. Had they survived I should have had great pleasure in recommending both Lieutenant Jones and Trooper Albrecht for the distinction of the Victoria Cross. I regret to say that both were killed before the conclusion of the action.

At 3.30 p.m., a storm of wind and rain of extraordinary severity set in and lasted for 3 hours. During its continuance the 5th Dragoon Guards, 5th Lancers, and 1½ squadrons 19th Hussars reinforced Wagon Hill, acting dismounted. About 4.45 p.m., when the storm was at its worst, the portion of our troops holding the extreme south-west point of the hill were again driven from their position, but were rallied and reoccupied it; 2nd Lieutenant R. E. Reade, 1st Bn. King's Royal Rifle Corps, rendering himself conspicuous by his gallant service at this period.

At 5 p.m., Lieut-Colonel C. W. Park arrived at Wagon Hill with three companies 1st Bn. Devonshire Regiment, which I had ordered up as a reinforcement, and was at once directed by Colonel Hamilton to turn the enemy off the ridge with the bayonet. The Devons dashed forward and gained a position under cover within 50 yards of the enemy. Here a fire fight ensued, but the Devons were not to be denied, and, eventually, cheering as they pushed from point to point, they drove the enemy not only off the plateau but cleared every Boer out of the lower slopes and the dongas surrounding the position. Lieut.-Colonel Park went into action with four Officers, but he alone remained untouched at the close. The total loss of the Devons was nearly 28 per cent. of those engaged, and the men fired only 12 rounds per rifle. Captain A. Menzies, 1st Bn. Manchester Regiment, with a few of his men, accompanied the Devons throughout. He also was wounded.

I desire to draw special attention to the gallantry displayed by all ranks of the Imperial Light Horse, some of whom were within 100 yards of the enemy for 15 hours exposed to a deadly fire. Their losses were terribly heavy, but never for one moment did any of them waver or cease to show a fine example of courage and determination to all who came in contact with them.

I have already mentioned that about 3 a.m., the

south-east end of Cæsar's Camp was also attacked, as
well as the pickets of the Natal Volunteers in the
thorn scrub to the north of that hill. During the darkness the enemy succeeded in establishing themselves
on part of that end of Cæsar's Camp, but the precise
details of what occurred have not been made clear, as
nearly all the defenders of this portion have been
killed. It is believed, however, that taking advantage of
a general similarity of dress to that of the Natal
Volunteers and Police, and many of them having a
perfect command of the English language, the Boers
succeeded in deceiving the pickets as to their identity,
and were thus able to effect a surprise. As already
stated, I sent the 53rd Battery, Royal Field Artillery,
under Major A. J. Abdy, to Colonel Royston,
Commanding Natal Volunteers; and these guns, most
ably handled, came into action on the Klip River
flats, and, though exposed to the fire of several Boer
guns (including a 6-inch Creusot gun on Bulwana
Mountain), to which they had no means of replying,
shelled the south-east portion of Cæsar's Camp with
great effect, and inflicted very heavy losses on the
enemy. The 2nd Bn. Gordon Highlanders and 2nd
Bn. Rifle Brigade were sent to Lieut.-Colonel A. E.
R. Curran, who was in command here, and were
gradually pushed into the fight, company by company
wherever their services were most required. Gradually
the Boers were pushed back over the crest line, but
held on most stubbornly to the slopes, being continually reinforced or relieved from the dongas below
and from the adjacent hills, whence a fire of very

great intensity was kept up, while the whole of the plateau was swept by the Boer long-range guns from distant eminences. At last, after 15 hours of stubborn resistance by our men, and of continual effort on the part of the Boers, the enemy were driven off at all points during the same storm in which Wagon Hill was also cleared as already described, their retreat being hastened by the heavy fire poured on them as they retired.

Another attack was made before dawn on the 6th January on Observation Hill West, occupied by ½ battalion 1st Bn. Devonshire Regiment, under Major M. C. Curry. The enemy gained some dead ground near our works during the darkness, and at 9.30 a.m., and again at a later hour, they attempted to storm the works under cover of the fire of these men and of guns and rifles from all the surrounding kopjes. These, however, were repelled with no great difficulty by the wing 1st Bn. Devonshire Regiment, and the Artillery allotted to this portion of the defence, consisting of Royal Field Artillery and naval guns. The enemy, however, held on to the dead ground originally occupied all day, and only withdrew during the storm in the afternoon. The remainder of Section "B" and the whole of Section "A" of the defences were subjected to a heavy fire of guns and rifles all day, but no other attempt to press home an attack was made on these portions of our line.

Our losses, I regret to say, were very heavy, consisting of 14 Officers and 135 non-commissioned officers and men killed, and 31 officers and 244 men wounded. I have not been able to ascertain the actual loss to the Boers, but 79 bodies found within our lines were returned to them next day for burial, and native spies report that their total casualties could not be less than 700.

On 8th January a thanksgiving service in commemoration of the repulse of the enemy on 6th idem was held by Archdeacon Barker, and very largely attended by such officers and men as could be spared from duty. From this time until the end of the siege, no further effort to carry Ladysmith by assault was made by the Boers, whose attention was fully occupied by the various attacks made by Sir Redvers Buller on the line of the Tugela, though the town and camps were exposed to a daily bombardment from the enemy's guns, and skirmishing between our outposts and those of the Boers went on all day and every day, and caused us small but continuous losses. During this period I shall only refer to a night enterprise undertaken by 2nd Lieutenant H. C. W. Theobald, and 15 non-commissioned officers and men, 1st Bn. Gloucestershire Regiment. The object was to set fire to the abbattis which the enemy had constructed at the foot of Gun Hill, and was carried out in a manner reflecting credit on the young Officer in command, and without loss; while creating a considerable scare among the Boers who fired heavily in the darkness for a considerable time.

On 1st March I sent Colonel W. G. Knox, with the 1st Bn. Liverpool Regiment, 1st Bn. Devonshire Regiment, 2nd Bn. Gordon Highlanders, 5th

Dragoon Guards, and the 53rd and 67th Batteries, Royal Field Artillery, to move out along the Newcastle Road to harass as much as possible the enemy whom we could see retiring before the successful advance of Sir Redvers Buller's force. Colonel Knox carried Long Hill and Pepworth Hill and opened fire with his guns on Modder Spruit Railway Station and the large Boer camp there, which the enemy at once evacuated. Both men and horses were too weak for rapid or prolonged operations, but several of the enemy's camps were captured, and the force returned after having very successfully carried out their object to as great a distance as their weakness permitted them to pursue. Our casualties were 2 officers and 6 non-commissioned officers and men wounded.

Colonel Lord Dundonald with a body of Colonial troops rode into Ladysmith on the evening of 28th February, and on 1st March General Sir Redvers Buller himself arrived, and the siege came to an end.

VII

During the period from 6th January to 1st March, our struggle became one against disease and starvation even more than against the enemy. Our worst foes in this respect were enteric fever and dysentery, the former especially committing great ravages among the young soldiers of the garrison. Our deaths by disease from 2nd November, 1899, to 28th February, 1900, amounted to 12 officers and 529 non-commissioned officers and men. The officers of the Royal Army Medical Corps, the Army Nursing Sisters, the many ladies who voluntarily offered their services as nurses, and the hospital staffs of all ranks, maintained throughout the siege a brave and protracted struggle against sickness under almost every possible disadvantage, their numbers being most inadequate for the work to be done, and the supplies of drugs and of suitable food for invalids being entirely insufficient for so many patients for so long a period.

Even more important was the regulation and augmentation of the food supplies, as will be realised from the simple statement that 21,000 mouths had to be fed for 120 days; and the admirable manner in which all arrangements were made and carried out by the Officers of the Army Service Corps and Indian Commissariat Department under the able and untiring superintendence of Colonel E. W. D. Ward, C.B., my A.A.G. (B), will be evident from the fact that at the date of the relief we still possessed resources capable of maintaining this great number on reduced rations for another 30 days.

At the commencement of the siege, it became necessary to augment as far as possible all food supplies, and, with this view, one mill and subsequently two, were taken over and worked under military supervision and with labour and mechanics obtained from the employés of the Natal Government Railway, who remained voluntarily with the garrison. From these mills we produced during the siege mealie flour, mealie bran and crushed mealies. The mills were worked under the personal supervision of Lieut.-Colonel Stoneman, A.S.C., D.A.A.G., assisted by Major D. M. Thompson, Assistant Commissary-General, Indian Commissariat Transport Department.

When grazing and forage became scarce and the supply of cattle approached within a measurable distance of extinction, it was necessary to utilise for food the horses which would otherwise have died from exhaustion and weakness. From these slaughtered horses very considerable additions to the food supply were made, by the establishment of a factory from which were made: (i.) "Chevril," a strong meat soup issued nightly to the troops; (ii.) a condensed form of "Chevril" which took the place in the hospitals of various meat extracts which had been expended; (iii.) a jelly similar to calf-foot jelly for the sick and wounded; (iv.) "Chevril paste" made of boiled meat and jelly and issued as a ration to the men, and which being similar to the potted meats manufactured at home was much appreciated by the troops; and finally (v.) "neats-foot oil," which was used for lubricating the heavy Naval Ordnance. The boiled meat was given to the soldiers at the rate of 1/2 lb. per man.

The whole of this factory was under the management of Lieutenant C. E. J. MacNalty, A.S.C., whose untiring energy, ingenuity, and intelligence are deserving of high commendation. Captain J. R. Young, R.E., R.S.O., converted a railway locomotive shed into a factory, and displayed very great skill in improvising the various appliances necessary for the manufacture of the different foods.

With the object of still further improving the rations a sausage factory was established which converted the horse-flesh into excellent sausages, issued to the men at the rate of 1/4 lb. per head. This factory was most efficiently worked under the supervision of Mr. R. Beresford Turner.

As a safeguard against any serious loss of animals by disease or from other causes with a consequent reduction of our power of continuing the defence, a reserve of "biltong" was prepared, under the superintendence of Captain A. Long, A.S.C., who undertook it in addition to his onerous duties of Local Transport Officer.

The very large number of enteric and dysentery patients rendered it necessary to utilise all available sources of milk supply. All milch cows were requisitioned, and a dairy system established which provided milk, on medical certificate, for the sick, both military and civilian.

The feeding of the civil population was carried out by the Army Service Corps, a staff of civilian assistants being organised for distribution, and a large shed specially converted for the purpose. The two foregoing duties were carried out under the direction of Lieut.-Colonel Stoneman, D.A.A.G., and Major Thompson, A.C.G.

On the investment of Ladysmith, the main was broken by the enemy, and the water supply for the camp and town became dependent upon the Klip River. A system of filtration by Berkefeld filters was commenced, which answered well so long as the limited supply of alum lasted; as soon as it was expended the muddy condition of the water clogged the filters, and this method became unreliable. Three condensers were then constructed out of improvised materials by Mr. Binnie, Maintenance Manager, Natal Government Railway, under the able direction of Engineer C. C. Sheen, R.N., H.M. Ship "Powerful." As a further means of obtaining pure water apparatus for clearing water was constructed out of barrack sheeting placed on wooden stands, and having a deposit of wood ashes, through which the water was strained. It thus became possible to use the filters and also to provide all units with cleaning arrangements. It was possible, so long as the coal lasted, to supply at least 12,000 gallons of condensed or filtered water daily. The management of the water supply was carried out by Lieutenant H. B. Abadie, 11th Hussars, who performed the duties of Staff Officer for Water Supplies, and whose work is deserving of much praise.

Mr. W. King, District Inspector, Public Works Department, Mr. R. Brooke and the officials of that department, rendered most valuable assistance in every way possible.

With the object of reducing the number of orderlies employed in the conveyance of letters, a postal system, which included all the defences and the camp and town, was organised and most efficiently carried: out by Captain P. C. J. Scott, A.S.C.

In order to supply the deficiency of hay, a corps of grass-cutters was formed and placed under the charge of Major W. J. R. Wickham, Assistant Commissary-General, Indian Commissariat Transport

Department. This corps, which consisted of Indian refugees and Kaffirs, did excellent work, and collected grass under conditions of considerable difficulty.

I take this opportunity of publicly expressing my deep sense of the gallantry and patient endurance of hardships displayed by all ranks of all corps under my command.

The Naval Brigade of H.M. Ship "Powerful," under Captain the Honourable Hedworth Lambton, R.N., have rivalled the best of our troops in gallantry and endurance, and their long-range guns, though hampered by a most serious want of sufficient ammunition, have played a most prominent part in the defence, and have been most successful in keeping the enemy from bringing his guns to the ranges at which they would have been most efficient.

The Cavalry have not only performed their regular duties, but when their horses became non-effective have served as infantry, being re-armed with rifle and bayonet, and taking their regular share in holding the fortifications.

The Artillery have displayed their usual skill and gallantry, whether as mobile batteries or when used as guns of position in fixed emplacements as became increasingly necessary during the latter portion of the investment.

The Royal Engineers, both Officers and men, have sustained the grand traditions of their corps, and whether engaged on the defences, in maintaining telegraphic and telephonic communication between all sections of the defences, in ballooning, or in any other work required of them, have done everything which they were called upon to perform in a manner which has afforded me the highest satisfaction.

The work of the Infantry especially, exposed day and night to all weathers on our lines of defence, almost continually under fire, and living latterly on a ration consisting of little more than a proportion of horse flesh with 1/2 lb. per man of inferior and scarcely eatable mealie bread, has been of the most severe and trying nature, and has been carried out without a murmur and with the most cheerful steadfastness.

Of the Imperial Light Horse, specially raised in Natal at the commencement of the war, I have already expressed my opinion. No praise can be too great for the gallantry and determination which all ranks of this corps have invariably displayed in action.

The Natal Volunteers have performed invaluable service. Their knowledge of the country has been of the very greatest use to me, and in every action in which they have been engaged they have shown themselves most forward and daring. The Natal Naval Volunteers have proved themselves worthy comrades of the land forces of the Colony.

The civil inhabitants of Ladysmith, of all ages and both sexes, have uncomplainingly borne the privations inseparable from a siege, and have endured the long-continued bombardment to which they have been exposed with a fortitude which does them honour.

In conclusion, I trust I may be allowed to give

expression to the deep sense of gratitude, felt not only by myself but by every soldier, sailor and civilian who has been through the siege, to General Sir Redvers Buller and his gallant force, who, after such severe fighting, so many hardships, and notwithstanding very severe losses, have triumphantly carried out the relief of my beleagured garrison.

VIII

Telegrams concerning the Siege of Ladysmith.

MESSAGES BETWEEN SIR G. WHITE AND SIR R. BULLER.

From General Sir G. White to General Sir R. Buller.
(Received at Estcourt and telegraphed to Pietermaritzburg, 4th December.)

No. 20 P, 30th November. Flashing signals clouds seen last night for first time. Following portion only read:—"I do not yet know which way I will come.

How much longer could you hold out? From Maritzburg, from Buller." Commencement of message and date not read. Situation here unchanged; but enemy still mounting additional guns against some of our essential positions. I have provision for 70 days, and believe I can defend Ladysmith while they last. Hay or grazing is a difficulty; I have 35 days' supply of this at reduced ration. Small-arm ammunition, 5½ million; 15-pr. guns, 250 rounds per gun; 4.7-inch naval guns, 170 rounds per gun; 12-pr. naval guns, 270 rounds per gun; 6.3-inch howitzer, 430 rounds per gun. Enemy learns every plan of operations I form, and I cannot discover source. I have locked up or banished every suspect, but still have undoubted evidence of betrayal. Native deserters from enemy and our native scouts report enemy much disheartened by news of advance on Free State, victory on Mooi River, and consequent retirement north of Tugela River. With regard to road of advance towards Ladysmith, I could give most help to a force coming viâ Onderbook Hotel or Springfield, but enemy is making his positions on that side stronger daily. If force south of Tugela can effect junction with me, I believe effect will be immediate and decisive. At present cannot go large as I am completely invested, and must reserve myself for one or two big efforts to co-operate with relief force. It will be the greatest help to Ladysmith if relief force maintains closest possible touch with enemy. Hospital return—wounded, 225; dysentery, 71; enteric, 15; other fevers, 12; other diseases, 109. Additional portion of message deciphered—"If you hear me attacking join in if you can." Please repeat entire message. I will keep a good look out and do all I can. Repeat General Clery.

From General Sir R. Buller to
General Sir G. White.
(Sent by messenger from
Pietermaritzburg.)

No. 58, 4th December. Your No. 20 P, 30th November, received. I shall have concentrated 4 brigades of Infantry, 5 batteries of Artillery, 1 regiment of Cavalry, 1,000 mounted Volunteers, by 6th December, and shall attack. I cannot yet say which route, but will (? communicate) with you in several cipher messages before I advance. I shall also send by searchlight messages in clear, but they will be false ones sent in order to deceive enemy.

CORRESPONDENCE BETWEEN SIR R. BULLER AND LORD ROBERTS AS TO FURTHER ATTEMPT TO RELIEVE LADYSMITH.

From General Sir R. Buller, Natal, to Field-Marshal Lord Roberts, Cape Town.

(Received 26th January 1900, 12.3 a.m.)
(Extract.)

No. 169. Sorry to say I find this morning garrison had abandoned Spion Kop in the night. They lost up there yesterday General Woodgate dangerously wounded, and 200 killed and about 300 wounded, mostly badly. I have gone over and assumed command, and am withdrawing the flank attack to Potgieter's Drift, which I shall reach morning 27th.

I mean to have one more try at Ladysmith, but fear that a great portion of the force is not in good spirits.

From Field-Marshal Lord Roberts, Cape Town, to General Sir R. Buller, Natal.

(Extract.)   Cape Town, 26th January 1900.

Your No. 169. I am much concerned to hear that the Spion Kop position has been abandoned. Unless you feel fairly confident of being able to relieve Ladysmith from Potgieter's Drift, would it not be better to postpone the attempt until I am in the Orange Free State? Strenuous efforts are being made to collect transport, and I am hopeful of having sufficient to enable me to move on or about 5th February. If White can hold out and your position is secure, the presence of my force on the north of the Orange River should cause the enemy to lessen their hold on Natal, and thus make your task easier. Reports from Boer camp point to their being fagged and unable to cope with our Artillery fire. It seems therefore most desirable to maintain as bold a front as possible for the next 10 days.

From Field-Marshal Lord Roberts, Cape Town, to General Sir R. Buller, Natal.

(Extract.)   Cape Town, 28th January 1900.

Please let me know exactly what your plan is for the next try to relieve Ladysmith, and about what date you think it would be possible to commence operations. I am deeply anxious that Ladysmith should be relieved, but unless you consider that you have a reasonable prospect of success, it would, I think, be infinitely better for many reasons for you to remain on the defensive behind the Tugela, until the operations I am about to undertake have produced the effect which I hope for. Early reply requested.

From General Sir R. Buller, Natal, to Field-Marshal Lord Roberts, Cape Town.
(Extract.)

Spearman's Camp, 29th January 1900, 3.25 p.m.

My plan for next trial to relieve Ladysmith is to turn the Spion Kop position by the east, crossing the Tugela three times, and using a new drift just discovered, which makes all the difference by enabling me to reach a position I had hitherto considered inaccessible. I am only waiting for the Horse Artillery battery from India, and if it arrives I hope to attack Wednesday at 4 p.m.

The death rate in Ladysmith is now 8 to 10 a-day, and their hospital stores have run out, so delay is objectionable. I feel fairly confident of success this time, as I believe the enemy had a severe lesson last week, and are very disheartened, while we are all right.

One can never safely attempt to prophesy, but so far as my exertions can, humanly speaking, conduce to the desired end, I think I can promise you that I shall in no case compromise my force.

Please forward this to Secretary of State.

From Lord Roberts, by letter, Cape Town, 26th January, 1900.
(Extract.)

I recognize what a very difficult operation you are now engaged in, and I should have been pleased beyond measure to hear that you had succeeded in relieving Ladysmith. You will now know from my telegram of to-day that, if you are not confident of forcing your way there, it would, in my opinion, be better that you should abandon the attempt, until I am in the Orange Free State, but I consider it is most desirable there should be no retirement from the line of the Tugela, for, as I mentioned in my telegram, reports from the Boer camp point to the enemy being harassed by the strain thrown on them, as they feel they are unable to cope with our artillery fire.

Letter to Lord Roberts, Spearman's Hill, 4th February 1900.

. . . I have to-day received, per Captain Foot, your letter of the 26th January. . . . White keeps a stiff upper lip, but some of those under him are desponding. He calculates he has now 7,000 effectives. They are eating their horses, and have very little else. He expects to be attacked in force this week, and though he affects to be confident I doubt if he really is. He has begged me to keep the enemy off him as much as I can, and I can only do this by pegging away. . . . I do not think a move into the Free State will much affect our position here. . . . If you would tell me how you propose to advance on Bloemfontein—from where that is—I should be better able to say what I could do.

The above extracts are published at the desire of Sir Redvers Buller, to explain the telegrams which follow:—

From Field-Marshal Lord Roberts to the Secretary of State for War. (Received 6th February, 11.15 p.m.)
(Telegram.)

Cape Town, 6th February 1900, 6.30 p.m.
Following received from Buller:—

"I have pierced the enemy's line after a fight lasting all of yesterday, without many casualties, and I now hold the hill which divides their position, and which will give me access to Ladysmith plain if I can advance. I shall then be 10 miles from White, with but one place for enemy to stand between us I must, however, drive back enemy either on my right or left to get my artillery and stores on to the plain. It is an operation which will cost from 2,000 to 3,000 men, and I am not confident though hopeful I can do it. The question is, how would such a loss affect your plans, and do you think the chance of the relief of Ladysmith worth the risk. It is the only possible way to relieve White, and if I give up this chance I know no other."

The following is my reply to Buller:—

Ladysmith must be relieved even at the loss you expect. I should certainly persevere, and my hope is that the enemy will be so severely punished as to enable you to withdraw White's garrison without great difficulty. Let troops know that in their hands is the honour of the Empire, and that of their success I have no possible doubt.

The Boer War - Mafeking under siege, 1899-1900

To Game Tree Fort
(1000 yards)

To Fort Nelson (800 Yards)

To Col Plumber's HQ at Kanya (70 miles)

Defence Railway

Hospital Redan

Fort Dummy

MAFEKING
(Whites only)

Dixon's Hotel

B-P's HQ

Molopo River

Cape Boys Kraal

Fingo Location

Cannon Kopje

Strangers Location

To Ladysmith
(310 miles approx
South-east of Mafeking)

Boer Long Tom ('Old Creechy')
first position (3 miles)

Police Barracks
Protectorate HQ

Stone Kraal

Mackenzie's HQ

To Kimberley
(250 miles
south)

'Stonehenge' Kopje

Native Stadt

Hidden Hollow Ft

Fort Limestone

Molopo River

N

Fort

Telephone wires

4 mile covered trenches

Eloff's dawn attack on 12 May

Distance in miles (approx)

0   ¼   ½

PART TWO

∞◦◦∞◦

DESPATCHES RELATING TO THE SIEGE AND RELIEF OF MAFEKING

IX

From Field-Marshal Lord Roberts to the Secretary of State for War.

Army Head-quarters, South Africa,
My Lord,   Pretoria, 21st June 1900.

I have the honour to submit for your Lordship's consideration a despatch, dated 18th May 1900, with annexures and a letter dated 6th June 1900, from Major-General R. S. S. Baden-Powell, describing the siege of Mafeking which lasted from the 13th

October 1899 to the 17th May 1900, and bringing to notice the Officers and men, as well as the civilians and ladies, who rendered good service during the above period.

I feel assured that Her Majesty's Government will agree with me in thinking that the utmost credit is due to Major-General Baden-Powell for his promptness in raising two regiments of Mounted Infantry in Rhodesia, and for the resolution, judgment, and resource which he displayed throughout the long and trying investment of Mafeking by the Boer forces. The distinction which Major-General Baden-Powell has earned must be shared by his gallant soldiers. No episode in the present war seems more praiseworthy than the prolonged defence of this town by a British garrison, consisting almost entirely of Her Majesty's Colonial forces, inferior in numbers and greatly inferior in artillery to the enemy, cut off from communication with Cape Colony, and with the hope of relief repeatedly deferred until the supplies of food were nearly exhausted.

Inspired by their Commander's example, the defenders of Mafeking maintained a never failing confidence and cheerfulness, which conduced most materially to the successful issue; they made light of the hardships to which they were exposed, and they withstood the enemy's attacks with an audacity which so disheartened their opponents that, except on one occasion, namely, on 12th May, no serious attempt was made to capture the place by assault. This attempt was repulsed in a manner which showed that the determination and fighting qualities of the garrison remained unimpaired to the last.

In recording my high appreciation of the conduct of all ranks during this memorable siege, I desire cordially to support Major-General Baden-Powell's recommendations on behalf of those serving under his orders, and the civilians and others who co-operated with him in the maintenance of order, and in the care of the sick and wounded.

I have the honour to be,

Sir,

Your Lordship's most obedient Servant,

ROBERTS, *Field-Marshal,*

Commanding-in-Chief, South Africa.

From Major-General Baden-Powell, Commanding at Mafeking, to the Chief Staff Officer to Lord Roberts.

                           Mafeking,

My Lord,   18th May 1900.

    I have the honour to forward herewith my report on the siege of Mafeking by the Boers, from 13th October 1899 till the 17th May 1900, for the information of his Excellency the Field-Marshal Commanding in South Africa.

I have the honour to be,
  Sir,
      Your Lordship's most obedient Servant,
      R. S. S. BADEN-POWELL,
          Major-General.

I arrived in the beginning of August in Rhodesia, with orders—

- To raise two regiments of Mounted Infantry.

- In the event of war, to organize the defence of the Rhodesia and Bechuanaland frontiers.

- As far as possible, to keep forces of the enemy occupied in this direction away from their own main forces.

I had the two regiments raised, equipped, supplied, and ready for service by the end of September.

As war became imminent, I saw that my force would be too weak to effect much if scattered along the whole border (500 miles), unless it were reinforced with some men and good guns. I reported this, but as none were available I decided to concentrate my two columns at Tuli and Mafeking, respectively, as being the desirable points to hold.

Of the two, Mafeking seemed the more important for many reasons, strategical and political—

- Because it is the outpost for Kimberley and Cape Colony.

- Also, equally, for the Protectorate and Rhodesia.

- It threatens the weak flank of the Transvaal.

- It is the head-centre of the large native districts of the north-west, with their 200,000 inhabitants.

- It contains important railway stocks and shops.
- Also large food and forage supplies.

Therefore, I left the northern column in charge of Colonel Plumer, and went myself to Mafeking, and organized its defence.

Mafeking is an open town, 1,000 yards square, in open undulating country, on the north bank of the Molopo stream. Eight miles from the Transvaal border. White population, about 1,000.

The native Stadt lies 1/2 mile south-west, and contains 6,000 inhabitants.

The defence force:

700 whites, of whom 20 were Imperial Army, remainder Protectorate Regiment, British South Africa Police, Cape Police, and Bechuanaland Rifles (Volunteers). These were used to man the forts and outworks.

300 able-bodied townsmen enrolled as town guard. Employed to garrison the town itself.

300 natives enrolled as cattle guards, watchmen, police, &c.

Half the defenders were armed with L.M., half with M.H. rifles, with 600 rounds per rifle.

Total Numbers.

White men	1,074
" " women	229
" " children	405
Natives	7,500

Our armament consisted of—

Four 7-pr. M.L. guns. (All old.)
One 1-pr. Hotchkiss
One 2-in. Nordenfelt
Seven 303 Maxims.

To this armament we afterwards added—

One 6-pr. M.L. old ship's gun.
One 16-pr. M.L. howitzer (made in our own shops).

I had two armoured engines promised from Kimberley. I had armoured trucks made at Bulawayo and Mafeking. One engine arrived, the other was cut off en route by the enemy and captured at Kraaipan.

On the 13th October the siege began.

General Cronje with an army of 8,000 Boers and 10 guns, most of them of modern pattern and power, surrounded the place.

On the approach of the enemy we sallied out and, in a sharp little engagement dealt them a severe blow, by which they lost 53 killed and many more wounded, and which had a lasting moral effect.

During the first phase of the siege, October and November, General Cronje made various attempts to take the place. These attacks we beat off without difficulty in every case, and responded by sorties, varying their nature every time as far as possible, and making them so sudden and so quickly withdrawn as not to give the enemy's supports time to come up and overpower us. Of these "kicks" we delivered half-a-dozen, on 14th, 17th, 20th, 25th, 27th, 31st October, and 7th November (the Boers quote 14, but they include demonstrations and shelling of dummy forts, guns, and armoured trucks, &c., which we put up to draw their fire).

The enemy's losses in this period were very heavy as compared with ours—

Boers' losses—287 killed, 800 wounded.(These numbers are quoted from Transvaal newspapers, but must, I think, be exaggerated. I think that about 600 killed and wounded would be nearer the mark.)

Our losses—35 killed, 101 wounded, 27 missing.

Cronje having lost a month of valuable time at Mafeking, now gave up the idea of taking the place by storm, and moved off south for Kimberley with 4,000 men and 6 guns (leaving General Snyman with the remainder, viz, 3,000 to 4,000 men and six guns (including a 94-pr. siege gun) to invest us.)

Seeing then that we could not be relieved for many weeks, if not months, I took over into our own management all details such as hospital, municipality, police, treasury, post and telegraph, railway, native affairs, water supply, ordnance shops, &c.

I also took over all food, forage, and liquor stores, and native supplies, &c., and put everybody on rations.

I had disposed my garrison over what some of my Officers considered a rather extended perimeter (about 5 or 6 miles), but everything was arranged for drawing in our horns if necessary. However, in the event we were able to maintain our original position, and even further to extend it as became necessary.

The next phase lasted 3 months, November to January, during which Snyman pushed his works and trenches nearer to the place.

He also drew a cordon of natives around the whole.

His artillery kept up a continual bombardment on the town.

On our part, during January, February, and March, we pushed out counter-works and gradually gained point after point of ground till we obtained grazing for our livestock, and finally (after a hard tussle in the "Brickfields," in trenching and counter-trenching up to within 70 yards of enemy's works), we drove them back at all points out of range for rifle fire of the town.

During this period, owing to the careful and systematic sharp-shooting of our men the enemy's losses continued to be largely in excess of ours. 40 per month killed was admitted by the Boer medical officer.

In April the enemy withdrew the siege gun, and contented themselves with investing us at a distance, and shelling our cattle in the hope of starving us into submission.

On the 12th May the enemy made a bold night attack on the place, and succeeded in getting into the Stadt with their storming party, but we beat back their supports and surrounded the remainder, inflicting on them a loss of 70 killed and wounded, and 108 prisoners, including Eloff their commandant (grandson of President Kruger).

In the meantime, Colonel Plumer had near Tuli prevented a force of Boers from invading Matabeleland from the south. After their retreat the rising of the river made the border comparatively safe, and I called him down to defend the railway and the Protectorate border (which were already being held by a small force organized from Bulawayo by Colonel Nicholson).

Colonel Plumer accordingly pushed down the line, repairing it to within 40 miles of Mafeking, and pushing back the enemy who had been holding it. He then established himself in a good position 35 miles north-west of us, where he was in touch by means of runners and pigeons, was able to afford refuge to our natives escaping out, and he was also able to put a stop to enemy's depredations and to give security to the natives throughout the Protectorate, his force being too small to effect more till reinforced. His presence enabled us to get rid of nearly 2,000 native women and children, which materially relieved the strain on our food supply.

Early in May, he was reinforced by Canadian Artillery and Queensland Infantry, &c., and on 15th he joined hands with a relief column from the south under Colonel Mahon.

And, on the 17th May, the relief of Mafeking was successfully effected by the combined columns, after a siege of 218 days.

One of the most noticeable features of the long and trying siege has been the loyalty, patience, and good feeling which have prevailed throughout the community, civil, military and native. The steadiness and gallantry of the troops in action, and their cheerful acceptance of hardships, are beyond praise.

The ladies, and especially those who acted as nurses in the hospitals, displayed the greatest patience and fortitude.

XI

THE SIGNIFICANCE
OF THE SIEGE

A force of 8,000 Boers and 10 guns was contained at the first outbreak of war, and prevented from either combining with the Tuli column, and invading Rhodesia, or joining the forces against Kimberley. Cronje's commando was thus held here for a month.

From 2,000 to 3,000 Boers and eight guns (including a 94-pr.) were kept employed here for over 6 months.

The enemy expended considerably over 100 tons

of ammunition, and lost over 1,000 men killed and wounded, and had four guns disabled and one captured.

Large stores of food and forage, and general stocks, were prevented from falling into the enemy's hands.

Valuable railway plant, including 18 locomotives, rolling stock, shops, coal, &c., were saved.

Refuge was given to a large number of British from the Transvaal.

Most of the local neighbouring tribes, and all those of the Protectorate and South Matebeleland, remained loyal which they could not have continued to do had Mafeking fallen and they been at the mercy of the Boers.

Loss of prestige to Cronje's force, who had apparently expected to take possession at once on first arrival, and had had proclamation printed annexing the district to the South African Republic.

Eloff and 108 Boers and foreigners made prisoners of war.

During the same period the northern portion of my force under Colonel Plumer (in spite of its small numbers and the exceptionally difficult country and trying climate in which it was operating) succeeded—

In holding and sending back the enemy in their attempt to invade Rhodesia, *via* Tuli.

In holding the Bulawayo railway for some 200 miles south of the Rhodesian border.

In giving direct support and protection to the natives in Khama's and Linchwe's domains, and

Bathoen's and the Protectorate generally when threatened by the enemy.

In pushing down and repairing the railway in the face of the enemy to within 40 miles of Mafeking, and there establishing a place of security for our natives escaping from Mafeking, and collecting supplies ready to effect our relief in Mafeking on arrival of reinforcements.

A small column organized by Colonel Nicholson, from Bulawayo, with armoured trains, &c., held Mangwe, Palapye, Mochudi, &c., on the railway until Plumer's column was available for the duty.

The whole of the frontier force, north and south columns combined, numbered under 1,700, while the Boers during the early part of the campaign had between 9,000 and 10,000 out on their northern and north-western border. Country operated over, between Mafeking and Tuli, 450 miles in length.

XII

DETAILS OF THE SIEGE
(ARRANGED ALPHABETICALLY)

ARTILLERY.

Our so-called artillery should of course have been entirely outclassed by the modern high-velocity guns of the enemy, but in practice they managed to hold their own in spite of their using powder, shells and fuzes all made in our own shops.

The artillery and also the ordnance shops were under Major Panzera, assisted by Lieutenant Daniell, British South Africa Police.

Casualties.

	Killed and died of wounds.	Wounded.	Missing.	Died.	Accident.	Total.
I. Combatants.						
Whites						
Officers	6	15	1			22
N.C.O.'s and men	61	103	26	16	5	211
Total						
Whites	67	118	27	16	5	233
Coloured	25	68				83
					Total combatants	**316**
II. Non-combatants.						
Whites	4	5		32		41
Natives	65	117				182
Baralongs	264					264
					Total non-combatants	**487**

Total all casualties during siege, 803.

Out of 44 Officers, 21 were killed, wounded, or missing.
Out of 975 men, 190 were killed, wounded, or missing.

COMMUNICATIONS.

Local.

Telephone.—All outlying forts and look-out posts were connected up with head-quarters, under management of Mr. Howat, postmaster, and his staff. I was thus able to receive reports and issue orders for all parts of the defence instantaneously.

Postal.—To cover the heavy expenses of runners, and for the convenience of the public, postage was established at: 1d. for town, 3d. for outlying forts, 1s. for up country.

Signalling.—Heliograph, lamp and flag signalling was established for defence purposes by brigade signallers, under Major Panzera and Serjeant-Major Moffat.

Megaphones were also made and used in outlying trenches and posts.

Phonophores were also made and used on the armoured train, attached to ordinary telegraph lines.

Distant.

Runners.—Native runners were employed twice weekly, or oftener when necessary, to take despatches, letters, &c., to our northern column. They had to be highly paid, as the risk of capture and death was very great.

I was thus practically in touch with my force on the railway, and through them with Colonel Nicholson at the base, and Colonel Plumer's column at Tuli.

CIVIL ADMINISTRATION.

I established, for the trial of all cases not directly amenable to military law, a Court of Summary Jurisdiction—

Members:
Resident Commissioner.
Resident Magistrate.
Town Commandant.
Officer Commanding Protectorate Regiment.
Chief Staff Officer.

At first it was a little difficult to make the civilians appreciate the restrictions of martial law, and, as times grew more critical, there came a tendency to spread rumours and to grumble, this had to be stopped.

I also published some explanatory remarks and advice on the working of martial law, &c., and these steps had a most marked effect, obedience to orders and a good spirit thenceforward prevailed in the garrison.

COMPENSATION.

From the commencement of the siege careful record was kept of all shell fire damage to property, and claims of owners considered and assessed. Total assessed, £16,462. 10s. 2d. No promise was held out that Government would grant compensation, the proceedings were merely intended to assist the commission should one afterwards be assembled, and to protect Government against exorbitant claims.

A record was also made of losses suffered by refugees, in property, livestock, &c.

All livestock killed or wounded by shell fire was bought at a fair price and utilized for food, so that the owners have no claims on this head, at the same time the value of the animals is in many cases not represented by cash, and it would be far more satisfactory to the owners if they could be repaid in kind. This is a point which I venture to suggest be taken into consideration when dealing with the Boers after the war; a substantial fine in cattle would touch them heavily without leaving them destitute, and the bestowal of such cattle on deserving and looted loyalists would give great satisfaction and be far more acceptable to them, and less expensive to Government, than grants of money.

CORRESPONDENTS.

(Under Lieutenant the Hon. A. Hanbury-Tracy as Press Censor.)

These gentlemen gave a certain amount of trouble at first, as for the most part they were more reporters than correspondents. Further reforms in the matter of correspondents in the field are very desirable. The enemy derived a great deal of information as to our circumstances from the newspapers, not only the local ones, but also from the Colonial and English papers, in spite of a strict censorship on our part.

DEFENCE ACCOUNTS.

(Under Captain Greener, British South Africa Police.)

Expenditure during the siege.

	£
To labour	13,024
" " pay, local corps and trench allowance	20,777
" " pay, clerical and civil staff	3,543
" " foodstuffs, grain, rations, &c.	36,076
" " material, clothing, equipment, &c.	10,801
" " hospital staff, comforts, &c.	5,411
" " local transport	890
Total	90,522
" " payments other than defence, viz., frontier forces, special pay, &c	32,729
Total	123,251
Receipts.	
By foodstuffs, and grain sales	5,184
" " soup kitchens	3,242

	£
" " sales of Government property	442
" " local post office	238
" " dog tax	67
" " fines	127
Total	9,300
Weekly average expenditure in pay	1,550
Average receipts for rations	625
Soup	600
Total	1,225

DEFENCE WORKS.

(Under direction of Major Vyvyan, for town and East Front; Major Godley, West Front).

Scheme.—General scheme at first was to secure the town and Stadt by clearing front, laying mines, fortifying outskirts, &c.

Then to push out advanced trenches to drive back those of the enemy, and finally to establish a girdle of outlying forts.

The scheme included the provision of bombproofs and extensive covered ways, gun emplacements, drainage, &c.

In all some 60 works were made, and about 6½ miles of trenches.

The perimeter of the works at first was approximately 7 miles, latterly it extended to a little over 10 miles.

Nature.—Generally semicircular redans, but no

two works were similar in trace, they varied according to position, ground, &c. At first dug out and kept very low, latterly, owing to difficulties of drainage, long grass, inaccuracy of enemy's shell fire, &c., they were made more upstanding. Head cover was found to be essential. When trenches were near, steel loopholes had to be used, the ordinary sandbag and wooden ones being too good a target to the enemy.

Huts.—A good form of portable iron and wood hut was devised, and used for housing the garrisons of the forts.

ENEMY'S ARTILLERY—FIGHTING, TREACHERY, FIELD WORKS.

Artillery.—Guns employed—

> 1-94-pr. Creusot, 15-cm., 20-lb. charge.
> 2-7-pr. (Jameson's).
> 2-5-pr. Armstrongs' B.L.
> 1-12-pr. B.L.
> 1-9-pr. Krupp, B.L.
> 2 Q.F. 14-prs., high velocity.
> 2-1-pr. Maxims.
> Total 11 guns.

The 94-pr. fired 1,497 rounds, and the artillery altogether fired 2,000 rounds during the siege.

The damage done was very small, partly owing to the open nature of the town and lowness of our forts, but more especially on account of the want of intelligent directing of the fire.

Fighting.—The enemy's attacks invariably failed from want of discipline and pluck on the part of the men.

In the attack on Cannon Kopje they got within 400 yards, and even started digging shelter trenches, but when the men began to fall the rest retreated promptly.

The night attack on the Stadt, on 12th May, was boldly led by Eloff and a number of foreigners, and had their supports come on with equal pluck we should have had a hard task to drive them out, but as it was the supports were easily beaten off and the storming party surrounded.

Treachery.—The enemy fired on numerous occasions on our hospital, convent, and women's laager, although these were conspicuously marked with Red Cross flags, stood in isolated positions, and had been fully pointed out by me to the Boer Generals.

The women's laager was deliberately shelled in particular on 24th and 30th October, 27th January and 11th April.

The Red Cross flag was used to cover artillery taking up position on 24th, 30th, and 31st October.

Convent deliberately shelled, 16th October, 3rd and 8th November.

Our white flag, returning from a conference with the enemy, was deliberately volleyed, 17th January.

Field works.—The enemy's trenches were of a very good design, and made in well-selected positions. The typical trench or fort consisted of a chain of small chambers 10 feet square, partly excavated, partly built up with sandbags, having stout walls, loopholed to front and rear, the whole roofed in with corrugated iron and railway rails. Command, about 3 feet.

FINANCE.

(Under Captain Greener, as Chief Paymaster.)

I ordered all Government accounts to be kept settled up to date, so as to leave as little as possible for subsequent settlement; much work and confusion has thereby been saved.

The accounts were well kept by Captain Greener and his staff. An examiner of accounts was appointed to check accounts before payment, and also an auditor for the larger amounts.

Cash in bank amounted to £12,000., of which only £650. was in silver. Cash soon became scarce, because the public, especially the natives and Indian traders, concealed all the cash they could get, in anticipation of the place being taken by the enemy.

Paper money thus became necessary, and I issued coupons for 1s., 2s. and 3s. Ultimately gold also became scarce, and £1. notes were printed in cyanotype and issued; but they never got into real circulation as people kept them as curios to the extent of £700. 10s. coupons were issued with satisfactory result.

For the convenience of the men, and to get cash from the public, a "Garrison Savings Bank" was opened. Deposits amounted to £8,800.

	£
Total Government expenditure to end of May1	42,660
Total Government receipts to end of May	11,828

FOOD SUPPLY.

(Under Captain Ryan.)

Early in the siege, I took over all merchant stocks and put everybody on rations.

Beginning on the usual scale, I gradually reduced it to the lowest that would allow of the men being fit for duty. During the latter part of the siege no extras of any kind were obtainable. All lived strictly on the following scale:—

	At first.	Latterly.
Meat	1 lb.	3/4 to 1 lb.
Bread	1 "	5 oz
Vegetables	1 "	6 "
Coffee	1/3 oz.	1/3 "
Salt	1/2 "	1/2
Sugar	2 "	
Tea	1/2 "	
Sowens	1 quart.	

We had a large stock of meat, both live and tinned.

For livestock, we had to open up wide extent of grazing ground. We ate the fresh meat first in order to avoid loss from enemy's fire, failure of grass and water, lung sickness, &c.

The tinned meat we stored in bombproof chambers, and kept as reserve.

During the last 2 months, we were on horseflesh three days a week.

Our stocks of meal were comparatively small, but we had a large supply of forage oats. These we ground into flour, and fermented the residue into sowens (a form of porridge) and the remaining husks went as forage to the horses.

Fresh vegetables were largely grown within the defences, and for a greater part of the siege formed a regular portion of the ration.

The cost of feeding the troops was 1s. 3d. per ration, or, with fresh vegetables, 1s. 6d.; about 3d. below the contract price in peace. Civilians paid 2s., and women in the laager 1s. 2d.

All liquor was taken over and issued in "tots" to the troops on wet nights, and I think saved much sickness.

Natives.—For the natives, we established four soup kitchens at which horse stew was sold daily, and five sowen kitchens. Natives were all registered, to prevent fraud, and bought rations at 1 quart per adult, and 1 pint per child, at 3d. per pint.

Defence watchmen, workmen, police, &c., and certified destitute persons were given free rations. The kitchens so managed paid their own expenses.

They were under Captain Wilson, A.D.C., with Mr. Myers as cash taker and inspector.

FUEL

Coal.—300 tons available at railway store, was used for armoured train, ordnance foundry, pumping station, flour mills, forage factory, forges, &c.

Wood.—25,000 lb. weekly for bakery, soup, and oat-sowen kitchens, cooking, &c. Procured from roofs of huts in the Stadt, old wagons, lopped trees, fencing, &c.

Petroleum.—Asbestos stove made, but was not a success.

Patent fuel.—Cow dung and coal dust, mixed in equal parts and baked, produced 20 tons good fuel.

HOSPITAL.

(Victoria Hospital—70 beds. Base hospital).

Major Anderson, Royal Army Medical Corps, Principal Medical Officer.

Dr. W. Hayes (acted as Principal Medical Officer during first part of the siege).

Surgeon-Major Holmden, British South Africa Police.

Dr. T. Hayes, District Surgeon.

Dr. Elmes.

Garrison.

Force.	Commander.	Strength.	
		Officers.	Men.
Protectorate Regiment	Lieut.-Colonel Hore	21	448
British South Africa Police	Lieut.-Colonel Walford	10	81
Cape Police, Division 1	Inspector Marsh	2	45
Cape Police, Division 2	Inspector Browne	2	54
Bechuanaland Rifles	Captain Cowan	4	77
	Deduct missing at Lobatsi	1	26
	Total drilled men	38	679

Town Guard, 296 men (untrained).

Total garrison—44 Officers, 975 men.

From the above Town Guard was formed the Railway Division, 2 Officers, 20 men, under (local) Captain More.

The following commanded sections of the defence:—

Western defences, Major Godley.

Stadt and south-western forts, Captain Marsh.

Cannon Kopje and south front, Colonel Walford.

South-eastern works (brickfields), Inspector Marsh, at first, Inspector Browne, latterly.

North-east works, Captain Cowan

Town, Colonel Vyvyan, at first, Major Goold-Adams, latterly.

Head-quarters Staff—

Chief Staff Officer—Lord E. Cecil.

Deputy-Assistant Adjutant-General (B)—Captain Ryan.

Intelligence Officer—Lieutenant Hon. Hanbury-Tracy.

Aide-de-Camp—Captain Wilson.

Commanding Royal Artillery—Major Panzera.

Commanding Royal Engineer—Colonel Vyvyan.

HOSPITAL.

(Under Major Anderson, Royal Army Medical Corps, as Principal Medical Officer).

Staff—

Dr. W. Hayes (acted as Principal Medical Officer during first part of siege).

Surgeon-Major Holmden, British South Africa Police.

Dr. T. Hayes, District Surgeon.

Dr. Elmes.

Victoria Hospital (base hospital).—Nursing Staff: Miss Hill (Matron) and three nurses, assisted by four volunteer nurses; also by Mother Teresa and six sisters.

Convalescent hospital.—At convent, Lady Sarah Wilson.

Women and childrens' hospital—Miss Craufurd.

On outbreak of war I took over the town hospital, but at first the administration was not satisfactory on account of want of supervision over expenses of stores, and sanitation. I therefore appointed an issuer and storekeeper, and a sanitary inspector. To existing accommodation I added a native ward, nurses' quarters, a ward for Colonial Contingent, and a boarded marquee for shell wounds, &c.

Both doctors and nurses did excellent work, always shorthanded, and frequently under fire. (All the hospital buildings were struck by shells and bullets, and the first convalescent hospital was wrecked, and the second damaged by 94-pr. shells).

NATIVES.

(Under Mr. Bell, Resident Magistrate and Civil Commissioner).

Natives in Mafeking, during the siege, were—

Baralongs	5,000
Fingoes, Shangans, and district	
Baralongs	2,000
Total,	between 7,000 and 8,000.

The Shangans were refugees from the Johannesburg mines, and were sent into Mafeking by the Boers on the outbreak of war. Being accustomed to digging they proved useful for working gangs on the defences.

The district Baralongs, Fingoes, and Cape Boys, came into Mafeking when their villages were burnt and their cattle looted by the Boers. From among them we got about 300 men to act as armed cattle guards, watchmen, police, &c.

The local Baralongs living in the Stadt displayed their loyalty, and did some good service (especially after I had deposed their Chief Wessels for want of energy, and supplied good despatch runners, spies, cattle runners, &c.

Of the natives living in the district, Saani remained particularly loyal, and although a prisoner in the hands of the Boers he managed to send us information from time to time. Bathoen was loyal, but too timid to be of use. Copane, a subject of the Boers, although forced to supply them with men, offered us his allegiance. Hatsiokomo and Matuba (British subjects) joined the enemy, and the latter and his men fought with them.

RAILWAY.

(Under Captain More.)

132 men, 46 women, 86 children.

Eighteen locomotives, only one of which was damaged by shell fire, as they were moved round to the "lee" side of the railway buildings with every move of the enemy's big gun.

Also a large amount of rolling stock.

Value of railway plant, £120,000.

A defence railway 1½ miles long was laid round the north-east front.

We made three armoured trucks, walls of steel rails, iron lookout tower, acetyline search light, speaking tubes, electric bells, water, medicine chests, stretchers, &c.

200 tons of rails were used in construction of bombproofs.

The armoured trains did much good service.

SPECIALITIES.

Ammunition.—Mr. Fodisch, our gunsmith, reloaded Martini Henry cartridges, using ordinary gun caps fixed with plaster of Paris for detonators. Powder and bullets were home made.

Armoured train.—We armoured ordinary long-bogey trucks with steel rails (iron ones not being bullet-proof) to a height of 5 feet, with loopholes and gun ports. I had three prepared at Mafeking under the able direction of Mr. More, Resident Engineer

Bechuanaland Railway, also three at Bulawayo by Mr. Wallis, Resident Engineer.

Brawn was made from ox and horse hides and feet, and was much appreciated as meat.

Bombs.—Dynamite bombs were made up in small potted meat and milk tins for use as hand grenades, with slow match fuzes, with complete success by Lieutenant Feltham. Serjeant Page, champion bait thrower of Port Elizabeth, by using a whip stick and short line was able to throw these with accuracy over a distance of 100 yards.

Fuel.—When coal and wood began to run low a very satisfactory fuel was made up of coal dust and cowdung mixed.

Fuzes.—A simple and useful percussion fuze was invented by Lieutenant Daniell, British South Africa Police, in which the butt end of a Lee-Metford-cartridge was used as detonator. This fuze was in regular use with our locally-made shells.

Howitzer.—A 6-inch howitzer was made in our workshops, under the orders of Major Panzera, by Mr. Conolly. The bore was a tube of steel, with iron rings shrunk on in two tiers. The breech was a block of cast bronze. The trunnions and ring were a similar solid casting. The gun threw a 18-lb. ball (shell), and reached a distance of 4,000 yards.

Lookout poles.—Telescopic lookout poles were made of lengths of iron piping, and set up with steel wire stays, with a pulley and slung seat to hoist the man to the masthead. Height, about 18 feet.

Oat bread.—Mr. Ellitson, our master baker, made

up our forage oats into a good form of bread. The oats were winnowed, cleaned, kiln dried, ground, steam sieved (twice), and made into bread in the usual way, with a small admixture of Boer meal.

Search light.—Mr. Walker, agent for the Acetyline Gas Company, under Captain More's direction, made a very effective and portable acetyline search light with an engine head-light and a theodolite stand. These we had stationed in the principal forts and on the armoured train.

Signalling lamp.—Serjeant-Major Moffat and Mr. Walker devised a very effective and portable acetyline signalling lamp, which is reckoned to be readable at 15 miles. We had two in work.

Sowens.—This is a form of porridge, made from the fermented bran of oats after the flour had been extracted for making bread. 100 lb. of bran in 37 gallons of water give 33 gallons of sowens. On this food we fed both natives and whites. We had five sowen kitchens, each capable of producing 800 gallons daily. It was sold at 6d. per quart to those not entitled to it as a ration.

Sausages.—The horses which we used for meat were, as a rule, so poor in condition that we found it best to cut off the flesh from the bones and mince it for issue as ration. The remainder of the carcase then went to the soup kitchen. The mince was then mixed with spice and saltpetre, and made up into sausages, the intestines of the same animal being used for sausage skins. The meat thus treated lasted longer, and was more palatable.

Steel loopholes.—Finding that the enemy shot through ordinary loopholes at short distances, especially in trench work, I devised a form of steel loophole with two plates of 1/2-inch steel bolted together at an angle of 45 degrees, with a hole 2 inches square in the middle of the joint, the shield being 2 feet high and 2 feet wide.

Steel sap roller.—I also had a sapping shield made of two sheets of 3/8-inch steel, each 4 feet square, bolted together at an angle and mounted on wheels, to be pushed in front of a party pushing a sap under fire.

RELIEF COMMITTEE.

Numbers of the refugees and some of the townspeople, being without means during the siege, I formed a relief committee, consisting of the Mayor, the Base Commandant, the Chaplain, and other representative men, with myself as president, for disbursing funds for purchase of clothing and necessaries, &c., and for the issue of rations to deserving cases.

Sums received from England, from the various relief funds, were thus carefully and advantageously administered and accounted for, and there was no real suffering among the white population.

STAFF.

Head-quarters—
    Colonel Commanding—Colonel Baden-Powell.

Chief Staff Officer—Major Lord E. Cecil, D.S.O.

Deputy—Assistant Adjutant-General (B)—Captain Ryan, Army Service Corps.

Aide-de-Camp—Captain G. Wilson, Royal Horse Guards.

Intelligence Officer—Lieutenant Hon. A. Hanbury-Tracy, Royal Horse Guards.

Local—

Commanding Artillery and Deputy-Assistant Adjutant-General—Major Panzera, British South Africa Police.

Base Commandant and Commanding Engineer—Major C.B. Vyvyan, "Buffs."

Principal Medical Officer—Dr. W. Hayes (at first), Major Anderson, Royal Army Medical Corps.

Chief Paymaster—Captain Greener, British South Africa Police.

Town Commandant and Protectorate, Natives—Major Goold-Adams, C.B., C.M.G.

Local Natives—Mr. C. G. H. Bell, Resident Magistrate and Civil, Commissioner.

Women and children—Mr. F. Whiteley, Mayor.

Transport—Lieutenant McKenzie.

Post and telegraphs—Mr. Howat, Postmaster.

Chaplains—Rev. W. H. Weekes (Church of England), Rev. Father Ogle (Roman Catholic).

SPIES.

The enemy were well informed of all that went on in Mafeking during the siege. We had over 30 suspects in the goal for the greater part of the time, but it was almost impossible to get proofs against them. The stationmaster had undoubtedly been in communication with an ex-fenian, Whelan, a prominent member of the Irish Land League. This man we arrested on the outbreak of war, and kept in goal. He had among his papers a code for messages.

The natives acted as spies for the enemy; we caught two and tried them, and shot them.

More than half the families in the women's laager were Dutch, and of pro-Boer sympathies.

Four of our men deserted to the enemy at different times.

TRANSPORT.

(Under Lieutenant McKenzie.)

This department was very ably managed, and though at first much hired transport was employed, Lieutenant McKenzie gradually arranged so that the whole of the Army Service Corps, Royal Engineers, sanitary, &c., duties (as well as the regimental work) were carried out by the Government transport, available, viz.:—

11 wagons.
6 Scotch carts.
2 trollies.
3 ambulances.
188 mules.
12 oxen.

The mules kept their condition wonderfully well,

considering the absence of forage and the amount of work.

WATER SUPPLY.

(Under Major Vyvyan and Major Hepworth.)

The enemy cut off our water supply from the waterworks during the first few days of the siege. Fortunately the season was unusually wet, and consequently the Molopo stream did not run dry, and house tanks kept fairly filled. But to make sure against contingencies, and to ensure a supply of wholesome water, we cleaned out various wells and dug a new one of great capacity.

The water from these was issued to the town and garrison by means of tank wagons, filled nightly and posted at convenient points during the day.

WOMEN'S LAAGER.

(Under Mr. F. Whiteley, the Mayor.)

Formed at Mr. Rowland's house, where everything was placed at the disposal of the refugees in a most kindly way by Mr. Rowlands.

Number of whites.—10 men, 188 women, 315 children; also about 150-native servant girls.

Health fairly good considering the circumstances. Diphtheria made its appearance, but after four cases was stopped by isolation. Deaths, 24.

A large bombproof, 180 yards by 5 feet, was made for the accommodation of the whole of the inhabitants of the laager, with protected ways, latrines, &c.

The women and children were rationed, the supply and distribution being efficiently carried out by Mr. Whiteley, without any kind of remuneration to himself.

This gentleman carried out the entire management of the laager with conspicuous success, and was very ably assisted by Rev. W. H. Weekes and Mr. Rowlands.

The following were the cases dealt with by the Court of Summary Jurisdiction:—

Charges.	
House-breaking	14
Treason	35
Theft	197
Minor offences	184
Total	430
Punishments.	
Death	5
Corporal punishment	115
Detention in gaol	23
Fines	57
Imprisonment with hard labour	91
Total	291

XIII

ENGAGEMENTS OF THE SIEGE

ACTION OF 14TH OCTOBER.

Six miles north of Mafeking on railway.

Early in the morning of the 14th October our reconnoitring patrols exchanged shots with a strong party of the enemy, who were advancing along the railway 3 miles north of the town.

I ordered out the armoured train, under Captain Williams, British South Africa Police, to endeavour to rush the Boers and pour a heavy fire into them, as I wanted to make the first blow felt by them to be a really hard one. The train carried a 1-pr. Hotchkiss and a .303-inch Maxim, and 15 men, British South Africa Police.

I sent out, in support of the train, a squadron of the Protectorate Regiment, under Captain FitzClarence.

On coming up with the train he found it heavily engaged with the Boers, who had been strongly reinforced from their laager, some 7 miles north; they had also brought up a 7-pr. Krupp and a 1-pr. Maxim.

Captain FitzClarence dismounting his men advanced to attack with his left protected by the train.

For a quarter of an hour he was held by the enemy under a very hot fire, and then, pressing forward, well backed up by the train, he drove the enemy back and successfully beat off their several attempts to encircle his flank. Meantime, I sent up an additional troop under Lord Charles Bentinck, and also a 7-pr. These also became hotly engaged and did good work. The fire from the armoured train put the enemy's gun out of action before it had fired a shot, and eventually also drove the 1-pr. Maxim from the field.

The engagement lasted about 4 hours, and the enemy largely outnumbered our men, but Captain FitzClarence made up for this deficiency by the able handling of his men. Moreover, he kept his orders in mind, and when he saw the opportunity he got his wounded on to the train, and after driving the enemy back he withdrew his command quietly on Mafeking, covered by the train, without any attempt on the part of the enemy to follow him up.

In this their first engagement, the Protectorate

Regiment showed a spirit and dash worthy of highly-trained troops, and were most ably led by Captain FitzClarence and Lord C. Bentinck.

This smartly fought little engagement had a great and lasting moral effect on the enemy.

Their losses were afterwards found to amount to 53 killed (including four field cornets) and a large number wounded. They also lost a number of horses.

Our casualties were—

2 killed.

16 wounded (including two Officers).

1 missing (cyclist).

4 horses killed.

12 wounded.

ENEMY'S ATTACK ON THE STADT.

25th October 1899.

Enemy commenced shelling at 6.30 a.m. till mid-day from the east and south with seven guns. At noon they commenced a general advance against the town from the south-west, east, and north-east; the south-west being the main attack directed against the Stadt. Their number about 3,000. The enemy commenced firing at extreme range, to which we made no reply, reserving our fire for close distances. So soon as our volleys and Maxims commenced the enemy stopped their advance, and soon began to withdraw at all points. Casualties on our side were one man wounded, and two horses and eight mules wounded. The Boers losses unknown, but probably considerable, as their ambulances were on the field picking up for over an hour after the engagement.

It was afterwards (10th December) ascertained that the attack on the Stadt was intended as a feint while the main attack should come off to northward, on our western face. The Boers had expected the Baralongs not to fire on them, and so advanced more openly than they would otherwise have done; nor had they expected to find white men defending the Stadt. Their loss was, therefore, pretty heavy, and, surprised at their rebuff, they fell back altogether.

At one period of the action, a small mounted troop of Boers advanced at a gallop towards the western position, and came under fire of the Cape Police Maxim, which dropped five of them, the remainder rapidly dispersed.

During the afternoon some of our scouts near the Brickfields were moving, under fire, when one of them fell with his horse and lay stunned. Two Cape Police troopers in the works ran out and placed the injured man on his horse, and brought him in under heavy fire from the enemy: names, Troopers George Collins and W. F. Green.

NIGHT ATTACK ON BOER TRENCHES.

27th October 1899.

During past two days enemy had moved their advanced trenches closer into the east face. I determined to make an attack on their main advanced trench with the bayonet, in order to discourage their advancing further.

A night attack was therefore organized with Captain FitzClarence's squadron, Protectorate Regiment, supported by a party of Cape Police. Guiding lights were hoisted, by which Captain FitzClarence was able to lead his party past the flank of the main trench.

The attacking force moved off 9.30 p.m. in silence, with magazines charged, but no cartridges in the chamber, the order being to use the bayonet only. The men wore white armlets and used "FitzClarence" as their pass word. The night was dark, but still. The squadron attained its position on the left rear of enemy's trench without being challenged or fired at. Captain FitzClarence then wheeled up his men, and with a cheer charged into the main and a subsidiary trench, and cleared both with the bayonet.

The enemy's rearward trenches opened a heavy fire, to which the Cape Police replied from a flank, in order to draw the fire on to themselves, and so to allow Captain FitzClarence's squadron to return unmolested.

The whole operation was carried out exactly in accordance with instructions, and was a complete success. The more so as the enemy, being taken by surprise, were in much confusion, and, as we afterwards discovered, fired into each other. Their casualties, we heard on reliable authority, amounted to 40 killed and wounded with the bayonet, 60 killed and wounded by rifle fire. Our casualties were six killed, nine wounded, two missing.

Killed.

4323 Corporal Burt, 17th Lancers.
442 Trooper Josiah Soundy, Protectorate Regiment.
443 Trooper Charles Mayfield Middleditch, Protectorate Regiment.
171 Trooper Thomas Fraser.
202 Robert Ryves MacDonald.
222 Alexander Henry Turner.

Wounded.

Captain FitzClarence, slightly.
Lieutenant Swinburne, slightly.
Corporal Bernard Johnson.
Corporal Clement Adkins.
Trooper Arthur Bodill, severely.
Trooper Charles Donovan.
Trooper A. H. Hodgkinson
Trooper H. A. Dawson.
Trooper F. W. Hooper.

Missing.

Trooper Thomas Powell.
Trooper Franz Aurel.
The missing men were captured by the enemy.

ACTION AT CANNON KOPJE.

31st October 1899.

The enemy opened a heavy concentrated shell fire from the south-eastern heights, from the racecourse (east), and from Jackal's Tree (south-west), directed against Cannon Kopje. The fire was well aimed, and the racecourse gun took the work in reverse. For a time little harm was done beyond knocking down parts of the parapet and smashing the iron supports of the lookout tower: most of the garrison were lying in the trenches some 80 yards in rear of the fort. The gun and two Maxims in the work had been previously dismounted and stowed away for safety during shell fire, to which, of course, they were powerless to reply. The telephone wire was cut away early in the proceedings. After half an hour's steady and accurate artillery fire, the enemy, who had been gradually massing on the high ground south and south-east of the fort, began to advance in line of skirmishers from three sides at once; they were backed up by other parties in support. A large force also collected in the Molopo Valley, south-east of the town, and were formed evidently with the idea of storming the town after Cannon Kopje had been captured.

As the enemy began to get within range of the fort, the garrison moved up from their trench and manned the parapets and Maxims. It was then that we suffered some casualties from shell fire. As the enemy continued their advance, I sent to Captain Goodyear's Colonial Contingent to advance a party on to a ridge above them, and so to take enemy's attacking line in flank, but they could not be got to move.

One Maxim at Ellis's Corner now jammed, and I had to replace it by one from the reserve.

Meantime, I had a 7-pr. run out under cover of houses near south corner of the town. This opened, under direction of Lieutenant Murchison, on the flank of the enemy's line as it began to get near the fort. The gun made excellent practice, every shell going in among them and effectually stopped the further advance of the Boers.

These now hesitated and began to draw off, and as they did so their guns reopened on Cannon Kopje to cover their retirement. The fire then died down, and enemy sent our ambulances under Red Cross flags to recover their dead and wounded. We lost six killed and five wounded.

Killed.

Captain the Hon. Douglas Marsham.
Captain Charles A. K. Pechell.
2391 Troop Serjeant-Major William Henry Connihan.
Troop Serjeant-Major Hugh Bagot Upton.
2566 Trooper Arthur John Martyn.
2517 Frank St. Clair Traill Burroughes.

Wounded.

Quarter-Master-Serjeant E. O. Butler.
Corporal A. J. Cook.
Corporal F. C. Newton.
Trooper C. W. Nicholas.
Trooper F. R. Lloyd.

(The two latter died the following day.)

During this fight, the Boers sent out a Red Cross flag on to a commanding point and then brought their guns up into position there. I visited Cannon Kopje after the fight and congratulated Colonel Walford and his men on the gallant and determined stand made by them in the face of a very hot shell fire.

The intention of the enemy had been to storm Cannon Kopje, and thence to bombard the south-eastern portion of the town, and to carry it with the large forces they had collected in the Molopo Valley. Their whole scheme was defeated by the gallant resistance made by the garrison, and by the telling fire it brought to bear on them. We afterwards learnt that the attack was designed and directed by young Cronje. The enemy's loss was not known, but ambulances were seen about the field picking up for a considerable time, and native spies reported there was much mourning in the laagers, and that several cart loads of dead had been brought in and buried.

SURPRISE ON ENEMY'S WESTERN LAAGER.

7th November 1899.

At 2.30 a.m., Major Godley paraded his force, in accordance with a plan I had arranged, to attack the western camp of the enemy with a heavy fire at day-light, and then to retire again before enemy's guns and reinforcements arrived on the scene. The force in enemy's camp was reckoned at 200 to 250. Our force consisted of—

Two 7-prs.

One 1-pr. Hotchkiss, under Major Panzera.

One squadron of 60 men, Protectorate Regiment, dismounted, under Captain Vernon.

One troop of 30 men, Bechuanaland Rifles, mounted, under Captain Cowan.

The force moved out along the heights to about 1,500 yards in advance of Major Godley's position; Captain Vernon's squadron leading in attack order, with the guns on his left rear, and Bechuanaland Rifles covering his right rear.

At 4.15 a.m., our guns opened on enemy at 1,800 yards, and the squadron fired volleys by alternate troops into the enemy's camp, over which they had full command from the heights they were on. The surprise was complete, the enemy bolting in all directions to take cover. Their 1-pr. Maxim and 7-pr. Krupp in the Beacons Fort in a short time responded with a heavy and well-directed fire. Large bodies of reinforcements very soon began to come down from the main south-west laager. Major Godley thereupon commenced with-drawing his forces, artillery retiring first; the Bechuanaland Rifles occupying Fort Ayr to cover the retirement, which they did very effectively against a wing of mounted Boers, who had worked round to our right flank. The enemy brought a very heavy musketry fire to bear on our force, but the retirement was carried out with the greatest steadiness. Enemy's strength, about 800 or 1,000. Our retirement was further covered by 7-pr. at the west end of the Stadt, and the Cape Police Maxim and escort. In the course of the retirement, our 1-pr. Hotchkiss upset and broke the limber hook; her crew, Gunners R. Cowan and H. Godson, very pluckily stood up and repaired damage with rope, &c., and got the gun away safely under heavy fire from enemy's 1-pr. Maxim and 7-pr. Krupp and rifle fire.

Three of enemy's ambulances were seen picking up their casualties after the action, and we afterwards learnt that they had lost a considerable number. On our side we had five men wounded, five horses killed, five wounded, and 36 cattle in the refugee laager killed and wounded by bullets.

Names of wounded.

Major Godley, slightly.

Trooper Hodgkinson, Protectorate Regiment.

Trooper J. G. Thompson, Protectorate Regiment.

Trooper P. J. Westdyk, Bechuanaland Rifles.

Corporal R. B. Christie, Cape Police.

On this day a commando of the Boers made a demonstration against Khama's men on the Limpopo, and opened fire upon them, but shortly after retired across the border.

ACTION AT GAME TREE.

26th December 1899.

The Boers' work at Game Tree, 2,500 yards north of town, had checked our grazing in that direction, and it commanded our line of communication northward. Some shells thrown into it a few days previously had caused enemy temporarily to vacate it, showing it to be a weak open work; this had been confirmed by reconnaissance by our scouts, but as the enemy had been seen strengthening it during the past few days, I determined to attack before they should make it impregnable. Accordingly, two squadrons Protectorate Regiment, supported by armoured train and Bechuanaland Rifles, were ordered to attack from the left flank of the work, under direction of Major Godley, while three guns and Maxim prepared the way from the right front of the work. This scheme was carried out at dawn on the 26th, the guns making good practice, and the two squadrons advancing in attack formation exactly as required. But on pressing home the attack a heavy fire killed or wounded most of the Officers and the leading troops. These succeeded in gaining the parapet, but the work was found to have been strongly roofed in and so closed as to be impregnable.

The attack fell back upon the eastern face, and pushed forward again on the southern face, but eventually had to retire with a loss of—

Captain Vernon.

Captain Sandford,

Lieutenant Paton and 21 non-commissioned officers and men killed, and,

Captain FitzClarence and 22 men wounded,

Three missing.

If blame for this reverse falls on anyone it should fall on myself, as everybody concerned did their part of the work thoroughly well, and exactly in accordance with the orders I had issued. Both Officers and men worked with splendid courage and spirit.

BOERS' ATTACK.

12th May 1900.

At about 4 a.m. on 12th May, a very heavy long-range musketry fire was opened on the town from east, north-east, and south-east. I sounded the alarm, and the garrison stood to arms. The fire continued for half-an-hour; I thereupon wired to the south-west outposts to be on the lookout.

At about 4.30, 300 Boers made a rush through the western outposts and got into the Stadt; this they then set fire to. I ordered the western defenders to close in so as to prevent any supports from coming in after the leading body, and sent the reserve squadron there to assist. They succeeded in driving off an attack of about 500 without difficulty, and returned to round up their station. In the meantime the Boers in the Stadt had rushed the British South African Police fort and made prisoners the men in it, viz., three Officers and 15 men, staff of the Protectorate Regiment.

In the darkness the attackers had got divided up into three parties, and as it got light we were able to further separate these from each other, and to surround and attack them in detail. The first party surrendered, the second were driven out with loss by three squadrons, Protectorate Regiment, under Major

Godfrey, and the third, in the British South African Police fort, after a vain attempt to break out in the evening surrendered. During the whole of the day, while the struggle was going on in the Stadt, the enemy outside made demonstrations as if about to attack, and kept up a hot shell fire on the place, but without palpable effect.

We captured this day 108 prisoners, among whom was Commandant Eloff, Kruger's grandson. We also found 10 killed and 19 wounded Boers, and their ambulance picked up 30 more killed and wounded. Our losses were four killed, 10 wounded.

Our men, although weak with want of food and exercise, worked with splendid pluck and energy for the 14 hours of fighting, and instances of gallantry in action were very numerous.

RELIEF OF MAFEKING.

16th–17th May 1900.

When relief became imminent, I formed a small force of 180 men and two guns, under Colonel Walford, capable of taking the field should it be desirable to make a diversion or counter attack during the probable encounter between the investing force and the relieving column.

On the evening of the 16th May, the enemy contested the advance of the relief column 6 miles west of the place. Colonel Walford's party moved out and demonstrated as if to attack the Boers in rear. This caused them to withdraw a 1-pr. Maxim which had been posted on the probable line of advance of the column, and also a number of men with it. This move left the road open for Colonel Mahon's force to come into Mafeking, which it did during the night without the knowledge of the Boers.

Early next morning, seeing that the enemy were beginning to move wagons from the laager, I pushed forward Colonel Walford's force at once to attack, ordering the relief force to join in as soon as possible. This had a good effect, as our guns opened on their advanced trenches and prevented them from getting their 5-pr. away, and our men from the Brickfields, moving up the river, took the trench in rear and cleared it, killing five Boers and taking their flag and gun. Meanwhile, Colonel Mahon and Colonel Plumer's guns came into action and shelled the enemy's laager with great effect, the Boers going off in full flight, abandoning several wagons, camp equipment, hospital, &c. Colonel Walford's men, who had been working up through the bush, quickly took possession and drove off the enemy's rear guard without difficulty.

The operations connected with the relief of the place have, I assume, been reported on by Colonel Mahon, but I would add that his clever move near Maritzani, when he shifted his line of advance suddenly from one road to another, quite unexpected by the Boers, entirely puzzled them, and disconcerted their plans. And again, after the fight outside Mafeking, when he bivouacked his column at nightfall, the Boers were prepared to renew the attack in the morning only to find that he had slipped into the place during the night, and was through the town and shelling their laager on the other side.

The whole operation of the two relief columns was exceedingly well conceived and carried out.

XIV

RECOMMENDATION OF STAFF AND OTHERS

STAFF—MILITARY.

Major Lord Edward Cecil, D.S.O., as Chief Staff Officer, was of the greatest assistance to me. He stuck pluckily to his work, although much hampered by sickness during the first part of the siege. He did a great amount of hard work in the first organization of the frontier force, and at Mafeking, his tact and unruffled temperament enabled our staff dealings with the

Colonial civilians to be carried on with the least possible friction.

Captain Ryan, Army Service Corps, as Deputy-Assistant Adjutant-General (B), proved an exceptionally capable and energetic Supply Officer. On his shoulders fell the whole work of feeding the entire community, garrison, non-combatants, and native, a duty which he carried out with conspicuous success (practically unassisted), as we took the food supply out of the hands of contractors and merchants; and he lost the services of his two chief assistants, Captain Girdwood, killed, and Sergeant-Major Loney, convicted of theft of Government stores. Captain Ryan's work has been invaluable, and has mainly contributed to the successful issue of the siege.

Lieutenant Hon. A. Hanbury-Tracy, Royal Horse Guards, as Intelligence Officer and Press Censor, has worked hard and successfully, and with tact and firmness in his dealings with the press correspondents.

Captain G. Wilson, Royal Horse Guards, as my Aide-de-Camp, in addition to his other duties, had charge of the soup and sowens kitchens, and did most useful work.

To both the above Officers I am much indebted for their willing work and personal assistance to myself.

Honorary Lieutenant McKenzie as Transport Officer did excellent work in the organization of his departments, and in the purchase of mules and material, &c. In addition to his other duties he acted as extra Aide-de-Camp to me, and was an exceptionally energetic and useful Staff Officer.

Major Panzera, British South Africa Police, as Commanding Artillery, showed himself a smart and practical gunner, endowed with the greatest zeal, coupled with personal gallantry in action. The great success gained by our little guns, even when opposed to the modern armament of the enemy, was largely due to Panzera's organization and handling of them.

In addition to these duties he acted as my Brigade-Major, and proved himself a most reliable and useful Staff Officer.

Major (local Lieut.-Colonel) C.B. Vyvyan, the Buffs, was Base Commandant, Commanding Engineer, and (for 3 months) Town Commandant during the siege. As such, he organized the Town Guard and defences in the first instance. To his untiring zeal and ability the successful defence of the town is largely due. He carried out a very heavy amount of work, practically single-handed, and with conspicuous success.

Major Anderson, Royal Army Medical Corps, throughout the siege showed untiring zeal, coupled with coolness and gallantry, in attending the wounded under fire in action, in addition to his eminent professional ability. Latterly, as Principal Medical Officer, his unfailing tact and administrative capabilities rendered his services of greatest value. The strain of his devotion to his duty told heavily on his health.

Medical Staff.—Dr. W. Hayes, Surgeon-Major Holmden, British South Africa Police, and Dr. T. Hayes. All worked with conspicuous zeal and skill under a never-ending strain of work; all of them very frequently under fire in carrying out their duties, even in their own hospital.

Nursing staff.—The work done by the lady nurses was beyond all praise.

Miss Hill, the Matron of the Victoria Hospital, was assisted by a number of lady volunteers, in addition to her regular staff, consisting of Mrs. Parmister and Miss Gamble.

Mother Superior Teresa and eight Sisters of Mercy also worked in the hospital.

Lady Sarah Wilson, assisted by other ladies, managed the Convalescent Hospital.

Miss Craufurd managed the Women and Children's Hospital.

The above ladies worked with the greatest zeal and self devotion throughout the siege. The protracted strain of heavy work, frequently carried out under fire (Lady Sarah Wilson was wounded), told on most of them, Miss Hill being at one time prostrated by overwork. It was largely due to their unremitting devotion and skill that the wounded, in so many cases, made marvellous recoveries, and the health of the garrison remained so good.

Captain Greener, Paymaster, British South Africa Police, as Chief Paymaster, rendered most efficient and valuable service throughout the siege. He kept account of all Government expenditures and receipts connected with defence, feeding population, &c., in addition to his ordinary police and administrative accounts. By his care and zeal I am convinced that the Government were saved much expense.

REGIMENTAL.

Lieut.-Colonel Hore, Staffordshire Regiment, raised, organized, and commanded the Protectorate Regiment, which did invaluable service in the siege.

Major Godley, Royal Dublin Fusiliers, as Adjutant of the Protectorate Regiment, had much to do with the successful organization of the corps when it was first raised. As commander of the western defences of Mafeking throughout the siege, his services were of the highest value. His coolness, readiness of resource, and tactfulness in dealing with the Colonials, made him an ideal Officer for such command in action.

He was my right hand in the defence. I cannot speak too highly of his good work.

Colonel Walford, British South Africa Police, commanded the southern defences, with his detachment of British South Africa Police, throughout the siege with conspicuous success. Always cool and quick to see what was wanted, his services were most valuable.

Inspector Browne, Cape Police, commanded the detachment of Division 2, Cape Police. He and the splendid lot of men under his command did excellent work throughout the siege, especially in the occupation of the trenches in the Brickfields, where for over a month they were within close range of the enemy's works, and constantly on the alert and under fire.

Inspector Marsh, Cape Police, Division 1, commanded the detachment of Division 1 throughout the siege, and carried out his duties most efficiently and zealously.

Captain Cowan, commanding the Bechuanaland Rifles (Volunteers), had his corps in such a condition of efficiency as enabled me to employ them in all respects as regular troops. He was at all times ready and zealous in the performance of any duty assigned to him.

(Local) Captain More, Resident Railway Engineer, organized most effectively the railway employés into a paid division for the armoured train, and a division for the Town Guard. He managed their rationing, hospital, defence works, protection for their women and children, &c., in a most practical manner. His energy and resourcefulness were conspicuous throughout the siege. The armoured trains, defence railway, search light, &c., were made under his supervision.

Captain Marsh, Royal West Kent Regiment, commanded a squadron of the Protectorate Regiment, with very good results. He also had charge of the defence of the native Stadt, and displayed great tact and patience in his successful management of the natives.

Captain Vernon, King's Royal Rifle Corps, was a most successful Officer in command of a squadron, and displayed the greatest gallantry in action. He was killed in action on 26th December.

Captain FitzClarence, Royal Fusiliers, commanded a squadron in the Protectorate Regiment. He distinguished himself on numerous occasions during the siege by his personal gallantry and exceptional soldierly qualities. He was twice wounded. I have reported more specially on his good work in a separate letter.

Lieutenant (local Captain) Lord C. Bentinck, 9th Lancers, commanded a squadron of the Protectorate Regiment, with very good results. He did good service by his zeal and readiness in action.

The following Officers also did much good and useful work:—

Captain A. Williams, British South Africa Police.
Captain Scholfield, British South Africa Police.
Lieutenant Daniells, British South Africa Police.
Lieutenant Holden, Protectorate Regiment.
Lieutenant Greenfield, Protectorate Regiment.
Lieutenant Feltham, Protectorate Regiment.

Corporal (local Lieutenant) Currie, City Police, did exceptionally good service in command of the Colonial Contingent, to which he succeeded when Captain Goodyear (who originally raised the corps) was severely wounded while gallantly leading his men.

The following organized and commanded with most satisfactory results the native cattle guards, watchmen, &c.

(Local) Captain McKenzie, Zulus, &c.

Mr. D. Webster, Fingoes.

Corporal (local Serjeant) Abrams, Cape Police, Baralongs.

These detachments all did most useful and loyal work at different times during the siege in spite of their privations.

Town Guard.

Major Goold-Adams, C.B., C.M.G., Resident Commissioner of the Protectorate, commanded the Town Guard during the last half of the siege. His extensive knowledge of the country and people (both native and white) was of the greatest value, and his advice was always most willingly at my disposal. I am greatly indebted for the great assistance he at all times afforded me. The fact that the natives of the Protectorate remained loyal to us at a very critical time is due in a great measure to his advice and great personal influence over them.

CIVIL.

Mr. C. G. H. Bell, Resident Magistrate and Civil Commissioner, had entire charge of native affairs, and he managed the chiefs with great tact, and very successfully, at a critical time when they were inclined to sit on the fence and see which side was going to win, and were being tempted with offers from the Boers. As magistrate, he also rendered me great assistance during the siege.

Mr. F. Whiteley, Mayor of Mafeking. This gentleman's services were invaluable during the siege. In a most public-spirited manner he took up at my request, the difficult task of arranging for the feeding and housing of all the women and children, and carried out their management with marked success throughout the siege, devoting himself to the task without any return whatever.

He was much assisted by Mr. Rowlands, who gave up his house, garden, water supply, &c., to be used by the laager similarly without drawing any kind of compensation or return.

The Rev. Mr. W. H. Weekes also rendered valuable service in assisting in the management of the women's laager, &c.

Mr. Howat, Post and Telegraph Master, with his staff, namely—

Messrs. Campbell, Simpson, and McLeod did invaluable work in connecting up, and in keeping in communication with head-quarters the whole of the defence works by telephone. Their duties were unceasing, by night as well as by day, and were frequently carried out under heavy fire and at great personal risk. The zeal, energy, and willingness displayed by these officers was most conspicuous throughout the siege, and their work had a large share in bringing about the successful issue of the siege.

Mr. Heal, the jailer, carried out most arduous and difficult duties most loyally and efficiently. In addition to ordinary prisoners, he had in his charge military offenders, and also a large number of Dutch suspects, spies, and Irish traitors.

He was unfortunately killed by a shell, 12th May, at his post in the jail.

Serjeant Stewart, Cape Police, rendered valuable service as head of the civil police during the siege.

Mr. Millar, head of the refugees' laager, displayed much zeal and did excellent work in the management of the refugees' laager and defences, &c.

NON-COMMISSIONED OFFICERS AND MEN.

Trooper (local Serjeant-Major) Hodgson, Cape Police, acted as Serjeant-Major to the Army Service Corps, and was of the greatest help to Captain Ryan. He proved himself to be a most thoroughly reliable, sober, and upright man, clever at his work, and particularly active and zealous in its performance.

Serjeant Cook, Bechuanaland Rifles, specially recommended for clever and plucky scouting, and for gallantry in action (vide separate letter).

Serjeant-Major Moffat, signalling staff, for gallantry in action, in bringing a serjeant out of action under heavy fire. Also for good work as a signaller (vide separate letter).

Serjeant-Major Taylor, Colonial Contingent, for gallantry and general good work in the Brickfields, scouting, blowing up a kiln occupied by the enemy, &c.

This non-commissioned officer was killed in action.

CONCLUSION.

I should like to add that the conduct of the rank and file of the garrisons throughout the 31 weeks' siege, was beyond all praise. In all the long strain of privations, due to short rations and to the entire absence of all luxuries, as well as to living in the trenches month after month, there was no complaining, and the men took their hardships smiling. When there was fighting to be done they showed unexceptionable pluck and steadiness.

The Town Guard, formed of all the civilians capable of bearing arms, took to their duties as soldiers, and submitted themselves to military discipline with most praiseworthy readiness and success.

The self-devotion and good work of the ladies who acted as nurses in the hospitals, have already been alluded to, but the bravery and patience of all the women and elder children, under all the cruel dangers, anxieties, and privations to which they were exposed, were most exemplary.

The natives took their share in the defence of their Stadt, and showed great patience under their trials.

The notable feature of the siege was that the whole community was pervaded by a spirit of loyal endurance and cheery goodfeeling, under which all the usual local and private differences were sunk in the one great idea of maintaining Her Majesty's supremacy to the end. With such spirit to work on, the task of conducting the defence was an easy one.

R. S. S. BADEN-POWELL.

From Major-General Baden Powell, Commanding North-West Frontier Forces, to the Chief Staff Officer to Field-Marshal Lord Roberts, V.C.

Ottoshoop,
6th June 1900.

Other titles in the series

John Profumo and Christine Keeler, 1963

"The story must start with Stephen Ward, aged fifty. The son of a clergymen, by profession he was an osteopath ... his skill was very considerable and he included among his patients many well-known people ... Yet at the same time he was utterly immoral."

The Backdrop

The beginning of the '60s saw the publication of 'Lady Chatterley's Lover' and the dawn of sexual and social liberation as traditional morals began to be questioned and in some instances swept away.

The Book

In spite of the spiralling spate of recent political falls from grace, The Profumo Affair remains the biggest scandal ever to hit British politics. The Minister of War was found to be having an affair with a call girl who had associations with a Russian Naval Officer at the height of the Cold War. There are questions of cover-up, lies told to Parliament, bribery and stories sold to the newspapers. Lord Denningís superbly written report into the scandal describes with astonishment and fascinated revulsion the extraordinary sexual behaviour of the ruling classes. Orgies, naked bathing, sado-masochistic gatherings of the great and good and ministers and judges cavorting in masks are all uncovered.

ISBN 0 11 702402 3

The Loss of the Titanic, 1912

"From 'Mesabe' to 'Titanic' and all east bound ships. Ice report in Latitude 42N to 41.25N; Longitude 49 to 50.30W. Saw much Heavy Pack Ice and a great number of Large Icebergs. Also Field Ice. Weather good. Clear."

The Backdrop
The watchwords were 'bigger, better, faster, more luxurious' as builders of ocean-going vessels strove to outdo each other as they raced to capitalise on a new golden age of travel.

The Book
The story of the sinking of the Titanic, as told by the official enquiry, reveals some remarkable facts which have been lost in popular re-tellings of the story. A ship of the same line, only a few miles away from the Titanic as she sank, should have been able to rescue passengers, so why did this not happen? Readers of this fascinating report will discover that many such questions remain unanswered and that the full story of a tragedy which has entered into popular mythology has by no means been told.

ISBN 0 11 702403 1

Tragedy at Bethnal Green, 1943

"Immediately the alert was sounded a large number of people left their houses in the utmost haste for shelter. A great many were running. Two cinemas at least in the near vicinity disgorged a large number of people and at least three omnibuses set down their passengers outside the shelter."

The Backdrop

The beleaguered East End of London had born much of the brunt of the Blitz but, in 1943, four years into WW2, it seemed that the worst of the bombing was over.

The Book

The new unfinished tube station at Bethnal Green was one of the largest air raid shelters in London. After a warning siren sounded on March 3, 1943, there was a rush to the shelter. By 8.20pm, a matter of minutes after the alarm had sounded, 174 people lay dead, crushed trying to get into the tube station's booking hall. At the official enquiry, questions were asked about the behaviour of certain officials and whether the accident could have been prevented.

ISBN 0 11 702404 X

The Judgement of Nuremberg, 1946

"Efficient and enduring intimidation can only be achieved either by Capital Punishment or by measures by which the relatives of the criminal and the population do not know the fate of the criminal. This aim is achieved when the criminal is transferred to Germany."

The Backdrop

WW2 is over, there is a climate of jubilation and optimism as the Allies look to rebuilding Europe for the future but the perpetrators of Nazi War Crimes have yet to be reckoned with, and the full extent of their atrocities is as yet widely unknown.

The Book

Today, we have lived with the full knowledge of the extent of Nazi atrocities for over half a century and yet they still retain their power to shock. Imagine what it was like as they were being revealed in the full extent of their horror for the first time. In this book the Judges at the Nuremberg Trials take it in turn to describe the indictments handed down to the defendants and their crimes. The entire history, purpose and method of the Nazi party since its foundation in 1918 is revealed and described in chilling detail.

ISBN 0 11 702406 6

The Boer War: Ladysmith and Mafeking, 1900

"4th February – From General Sir. Redfers Buller to Field-Marshall Lord Roberts … I have today received your letter of 26 January. White keeps a stiff upper lip, but some of those under him are desponding. He calculates he has now 7000 effectives. They are eating their horses and have very little else. He expects to be attacked in force this week … "

The Backdrop

The Boer War is often regarded as one of the first truly modern wars, as the British Army, using traditional tactics, came close to being defeated by a Boer force which deployed what was almost a guerrilla strategy in punishing terrain.

The Book

Within weeks of the outbreak of fighting in South Africa, two sections of the British Army were besieged at Ladysmith and Mafeking. Split into two parts, the book begins with despatches describing the losses at Spion Kop on the way to rescue the garrison at Ladysmith, followed by the army report as the siege was lifted. In the second part is Lord Baden Powell's account of the siege of Mafeking and how the soldiers and civilians coped with the hardship and waited for relief to arrive.

ISBN 0 11 702408 2

The British Invasion Tibet:
Colonel Younghusband, 1904

*"On the 13th January I paid ceremonial visit to the Tibetans at Guru,
six miles further down the valley in order that by informal discussion
might assure myself of their real attitude. There were present at the inter-
view three monks and one general from Lhasa ... these monks were
low-bred persons, insolent, rude and intensely hostile; the generals, on the
other hand, were polite and well-bred."*

The Backdrop

At the turn of the century, the British Empire was at its height,
with its army in the forefront of the mission to bring what it saw
as the tremendous civilising benefits of the British way of life to
what it regarded as nations still languishing in the dark ages.

The Book

In 1901, a British Missionary Force under the leadership of
Colonel Francis Younghusband crossed over the border from
British India and invaded Tibet. Younghusband insisted on the
presence of the Dalai Lama at meetings to give tribute to the
British and their empire. The Dalai Lama merely replied that he
must withdraw. Unable to tolerate such an insolent attitude,
Younghusband marched forward and inflicted considerable
defeats on the Tibetans in several onesided battles.

ISBN 0 11 702409 0

War 1914: Punishing the Serbs

" ... I said that this would make it easier for others such as Russia to counsel moderation in Belgrade. In fact, the more Austria could keep her demand within reasonable limits, and the stronger the justification she could produce for making any demands, the more chance there would be for smoothing things over. I hated the idea of a war between any of the Great Powers, and that any of them should be dragged into a war by Serbia would be detestable."

The Backdrop

In Europe before WW1, diplomacy between the Embassies was practised with a considered restraint and politeness which provided an ironic contrast to the momentous events transforming Europe forever.

The Book

Dealing with the fortnight leading up to the outbreak of the First World War, and mirroring recent events in Serbia to an astonishing extent. Some argued for immediate and decisive military action to punish Serbia for the murder of the Archduke Franz Ferdinand. Others pleaded that a war should not be fought over Serbia. The powers involved are by turn angry, conciliatory and, finally, warlike. Events take their course and history is changed.

ISBN 0 11 702410 4

War 1939: Dealing with Adolf Hitler

The Backdrop

As he presided over the rebuilding of a Germany shattered and humiliated after WW1, opinion as to Hitler and his intentions was divided and the question of whether his ultimate aim was military aggression by no means certain.

The Book

Sir Arthur Henderson, the British ambassador in Berlin in 1939 describes here, in his report to Parliament, the failure of his mission and the outbreak of war. He tells of his attempts to deal with both Hitler and von Ribbentrop to maintain peace and gives an account of the changes in German foreign policy regarding Poland.

ISBN 0 11 702411 2

The Strange Story of Adolph Beck

"He said he was Lord Winton de Willoughby. He asked why I lived alone in a flat. I said I had an income and wished to do so … Two or three hours after he had gone I missed some tigers' claws and the teeth of an animal mounted in silver with my monogram."

The Backdrop

The foggy streets of Edwardian London were alive with cads, swindlers and ladies of dubious reputation and all manner of lowlife who fed on human frailty.

The Book

In 1895, Adolph Beck was arrested and convicted of the crimes of deception and larceny. Using the alias Lord Winton de Willoughby, he had entered into the apartments of several ladies, some of whom preferred, for obvious reasons, not to give their names. The ladies gave evidence, as did a handwriting expert, and Mr Beck was imprisoned. But an utterly bizarre sequence of events culminated in a judge who declared that, since he could himself determine perfectly whether the accused is of the criminal classes, juries should never be allowed to decide the outcome of a trial. The account given here is of one of the strangest true stories in the entire British legal history.

ISBN 0 11 702414 7

Rillington Place

The Backdrop

The serial killer, or mass-murderer, is often seen as a creation of modern society but quiet killers, drawing no attention to themselves in the teeming streets of the metropolis, have been responsible for some of the most notorious crimes of the 20th century.

The Book

In 1949, Timothy Evans was hung for the self-confessed murder of his wife and daughter at 10 Rillington Place, Notting Hill but their bodies could not be found. Two years later, a couple moved into the same ground floor flat, vacated by a man named Christie. They discovered bodies in cupboards, Christie's wife under the floorboards and Evans wife and daughter in the garden shed. Christie was convicted of mass murder and hung. At two subsequent enquiries, it was suggested that Evans may not have been a murderer. So, why did he confess?

ISBN 0 11 702417 1

Wilfrid Blunt's Egyptian Garden : Fox-hunting in Cairo

"Cairo. July 23, 1901 – On Sunday morning a fox-hunt was taking place near Cairo, in the desert, the hounds following a scent crossed the boundary-wall of Mr. Wilfrid Blunt's property, and two of the field, being British officers, who were acting as whips, went in to turn them back. Mr. Blunt's watchmen surrounded them, and, although they explained their intention, treated them with considerable violence."

The Backdrop

In the days of Empire, the British way of life was carried on with a blithe disregard for local peculiarities and this went hand in hand with a sometimes benevolent, sometimes despotic, belief in the innate inferiority of those under its thumb.

The Book

In 1900, the Imperial British Army occupied Egypt and, in order to provide sport for the officers who were kicking their heels, a pack of hounds was shipped out from England to hunt the Egyptian fox. Unfortunately, the desert provides poor cover and, one day, the pack, followed in hot pursuit by the officers, found itself in the garden of the rich and eccentric poet Wilfrid Scarwen Blunt. Attempting to protect the absent Mr. Blunt's property, his servants tried to prevent the hunt and were promptly arrested. Mr. Blunt objected to the officer's behaviour, both to the government and the press and the matter became quite a scandal.

ISBN 0 11 702416 3

R101: Airship Disaster

" ... about seven and a half hours later, shortly after two o'clock in the morning of October 5th, she came to earth two hundred and sixteen miles away in undulating country south of the town of Beauvais in France, and immediately became a blazing wreck. Of the fifty-four people on board, all but eight perished instantly in the flames ... "

The Backdrop

In the golden age of air travel, the R101 was the biggest and most splendid airship in the world. On the evening of the 4th October 1930 she left her mooring mast at Cardington on her ill-fated journey to India. As the ship ploughed on through increasingly threatening weather The Air Minister and his guests retired to their well appointed cabins. Seven hours later at 2.05 am her burning frame lay shattered on a hillside in France, 46 its 54 passengers killed instantly. The high hopes and ambitions of a brief but glorious era in aviation perished with them in the flames, changing forever the way we would fly.

The Book

As the shocked nation mourned, a Court of Inquiry was set up to investigate the disaster. Its report exposed the public pressure from the Air Minister, Lord Thomson, that whatever the technical causes of the crash had at the last minute unduly hurried designers, constructors and crew alike. The early end of the airship in modern commercial flight was the result.

ISBN 0 11 702407 4